Steck Vaughn

Maps Globes Graphs

Teacher's Edition

Level A

Contents

Meet your state standards with free blackline masters and links to other materials at
www.HarcourtAchieve.com/AchievementZone.
Click Steck-Vaughn Standards.

ISBN 0-7398-9107-3

© 2004 Harcourt Achieve Inc.

2 3 4 5 6 7 8 030 11 10 09 08 07 06

Harcourt Achieve

Rigby · Steck-Vaughn

www.HarcourtAchieve.com
1.800.531.5015

About the Program

Steck-Vaughn *Maps•Globes•Graphs* has been developed to teach important geography and social studies skills in a six-level program. Up-to-date, in-depth information in a self-contained format makes this series an ideal supplement to basal texts or an excellent independent social studies skills course. Clear, concise maps present new concepts in a straightforward manner without overwhelming students with too much information. As students develop practical skills, such as map interpretation, they also develop the confidence to use these skills. The features incorporated into the *Maps•Globes•Graphs* program were developed to achieve these goals.

Maps•Globes•Graphs consists of six student books with accompanying annotated Teacher's Editions. The series is organized as follows:

Book	Level
Level A	Grade 1
Level B	Grade 2
Level C	Grade 3
Level D	Grade 4
Level E	Grade 5
Level F	Grade 6

STUDENT EDITION FEATURES

◆ **Consistent formats** for each chapter include two teaching pages that introduce the skill, two practice pages, one mixed practice page, and *Skill Check*, a review page.

◆ **Geography Themes Up Close** introduces the five themes of geography—location, place, human/environment interaction, movement, and regions—in the beginning of the book. These themes are reinforced in five two-page special features that emphasize the concepts and relevance of the themes.

◆ *Map Attack!* and *Graph Attack!* features (in the three upper-grade books) build general understanding of interpreting map and graph information in a step-by-step format.

◆ **Vocabulary** words highlighted in bold type emphasize in-context definitions and increase understanding of the terms critical to studies in geography.

◆ **Glossaries** in each student book serve as both an index and a resource for definitions of key terms.

◆ **Atlas maps** in each book are a valuable reference tool for instruction and study.

TEACHER EDITION FEATURES

◆ **Annotated** Teacher's Editions facilitate effective instruction with minimal preparation.

◆ **Scope and Sequence** reflects key concepts of basal instruction for each grade level.

◆ **Teaching strategies** identify key objectives and vocabulary for each chapter and provide suggestions for introducing skills, teaching specific lesson pages and concepts, following up lessons with extension activities, and enhancing concept mastery with activities to complete at home.

◆ **Extension activities** involve both cooperative learning and critical thinking, and reinforce the concepts and skills taught in the program.

◆ **Geography themes teaching strategies** reinforce geography skills and vocabulary through lesson introductions, teaching notes, and extension activities.

◆ **Blackline masters** further supplement the activities available for use:

Map Attack! may be used with maps in a basal text or in reference materials.

Outline maps appropriate to each grade level may be used for skills practice in map labeling and place recognition.

Activities and *games* reinforce concepts.

Standardized tests in each level allow students to check their learning, as well as practice test-taking skills.

Steck-Vaughn Company grants you permission to duplicate enough copies of these blacklines to distribute to your students. You can also use these blacklines to make overhead transparencies.

◆ **Transparencies** provide full-color instructional aids. These transparencies may be used to introduce lessons, to reinforce key map and globe skills, or to review chapter concepts. These transparencies are perforated in the back of the teacher's editions for easy removal.

◆ **Letters to Families,** in English and in Spanish, are provided in each book. The letters invite families to participate in their child's study of the book and provide suggestions for some specific activities that can extend the concepts presented in the program.

SUGGESTIONS FOR PROGRAM USE

Maps•Globes•Graphs is easy to implement in any classroom. The following suggestions offer ways to adapt the program to particular classroom and student needs.

◆ Alternate the *Maps•Globes•Graphs* chapters with chapters in the social studies program. After presenting your first social studies chapter, present the first chapter of *Maps•Globes•Graphs*. When you return to the regular social studies program, apply any map skills learned to maps that appear in the curriculum. In this way, students reinforce their new skills in a variety of contexts.

◆ Set aside a specific time each week for map study. For example, spend half an hour every Friday on map study. Do as much in the *Maps•Globes•Graphs* Worktext® as time permits. Related activities, such as map show and tell, could be included in the map study time.

◆ Focus on a complete chapter of map study and cover the entire program at the beginning of the year, at the end of the year, or whenever best fits your class schedule.

The map and globe chapters in *Maps•Globes•Graphs* progress developmentally. For this reason they should be taught in the order they are presented in the Worktext®. However, the last chapter in each book presents several types of graphs, so this chapter could be interspersed with map chapters. In Levels D, E, and F, the graph topics reflect subjects covered by the maps and the basal programs. The graphs also can be used in conjunction with the graph presentation in mathematics studies.

 Meet your state standards with free blackline masters and links to other materials at **www.HarcourtAchieve.com/AchievementZone**. Click **Steck-Vaughn Standards**.

Scope and Sequence

Numbers refer to the chapters where each skill is first taught. These skills are reviewed and reinforced throughout the book and the series, as well as in the "Geography Themes Up Close" special features.

		LEVEL A	LEVEL B	LEVEL C	LEVEL D	LEVEL E	LEVEL F
Map Recognition	Photo/Picture Distinction	1, 2					
	Photo/Map Distinction	3	2		1		
	Map defined	3	2	1	1		2
Map Key/Legend	Pictorial symbols/Symbol defined	6	2	1	1	2	
	Labels	7	7	1	1	2	2
	Legend defined and related to map	6	2	1	1	2	2
	Abstract symbols		2, 3, 6	1, 3	1	2	2
	Political boundaries		6	1	1	2	2
Direction	Top, Bottom, Left, Right	4					
	North, South, East, West	5	3	1	1	1	1
	Relative location	4–7	3–6	1–6	1–8	1–5, 7, 8, 11	2–5, 10
	Compass rose		3	1	1	1	2
	Cardinal directions (term)				1	1	2
	Intermediate directions			1	2	1	2
Scale and Distance	Miles/Kilometers/Map Scale/Distance			2	4	3	3
	Mileage markers				5	4	4
Latitude and Longitude	Equator		4	7	7	8	1, 6
	Latitude			7	7	8	6
	Degrees			7, 8	7	8	6
	Longitude/Prime Meridian			8	8	9	6
	Estimating Degrees				7	8, 9	6
	Parallel					8	6
	Meridian					9	6
	Latitude and Longitude					9	6
The Globe	Globe	7	4	7, 8	7, 8	1	1
	North Pole/South Pole		4	8	7, 8	1, 8–10	1
	Continents/Oceans		4, 5	7, 8	7, 8	8, 9	1
	Northern/Southern Hemispheres			7	7	8	1
	Eastern/Western Hemispheres			8	8	9	1
	Tropics of Capricorn/Cancer					8	7
	Arctic/Antarctic Circles					8	7

		LEVEL A	LEVEL B	LEVEL C	LEVEL D	LEVEL E	LEVEL F
Grids	Grid Coordinates/Map index			6	3	7	4
Graphs	Pictograph			9			
	Bar Graph			9	9	12	12
	Line Graph			9	9	12	12
	Circle Graph			9	9	12	12
	Time Line			9	9		
	Flow Chart			9	9		
	Tables					12	12
Landforms	Types of Landforms		1	4	6	5	5
	Landform Maps			4			
	Relief Maps				6	5	5
	Physical Maps/Elevation					5	5
Types of Maps	Route Maps			5	5	4	4
	Resource Maps			3	1		9
	Special Purpose Maps				1	6	8, 9
	Combining Maps/Comparing Maps						8, 9
	Historical Maps					6	
	Climate Maps						7, 8
	Land Use Maps						9
	Inset Maps		7			3	3
Time Zones	Time zones defined					11	10
	International Date Line						10
Temperature Zones	Low latitudes					10	7
	Middle latitudes					10	7
	High latitudes					10	7
	Sun/Earth relationship					10	7
Projections	Projections defined						11
	Mercator						11
	Robinson						11
	Polar						1, 11

Geography Themes

OBJECTIVES

Students will

◆ recognize the five geographic themes: location, place, human/environment interaction, movement, and regions

◆ describe locations using relative terms

◆ identify the features of a place

◆ give examples of how people depend on or change the environment

◆ identify movement of people, goods, and ideas

◆ learn about regions

VOCABULARY

location   movement

place   regions

human/environment
    interaction

INTRODUCING THE FIVE THEMES OF GEOGRAPHY

In 1984 a joint committee of the National Council for Geographic Education and the Association of American Geographers published the *Guidelines for Geographic Education: Elementary and Secondary Schools*. This publication outlined five fundamental themes in geography—location, place, movement, regions, and human/environment interaction. These themes help geographers and geography students organize the information they gather as they study Earth and its people.

◆ **Location** is the position of people and places on Earth. There are two ways to describe location— relative location and absolute location. Relative location describes a location in relation to what it is near or what it is around it. One example of using relative location is by giving directions. How would you tell a friend to get to your house from the local library? Absolute location describes a specific address based on the intersection of lines of latitude and lines of longitude. The special feature on location is on pages 58 and 59.

◆ **Place** is described by physical features and human features. Physical features are natural features such as soil, landforms, climate, and plant and animal life. Human features are made or developed by people, such as roads, buildings, airports, railroads, playgrounds, and schools. The special feature on place is on pages 28 and 29.

◆ **Human/Environment Interaction** describes the interaction of people and their environment. People along coasts may depend upon the ocean for fishing. Human/environment interaction also describes how people change their environment. For example, a town might build a dam to prevent water from flooding the town. The special feature on human/environment interaction is on pages 50 and 51.

◆ **Movement** describes the way people, goods, and ideas move from place to place on Earth. Movement is the study of the interdependence of people; the linkages between places. The special feature on movement is on pages 14 and 15.

◆ **Regions** are a way to organize information about areas with common features. Geographers use physical and human features as criteria to draw regional boundaries. Some physical features used include climate, landforms, bodies of water, and animal life. Some human features used include land use, language, and population. The special feature on regions is on pages 42 and 43.

TEACHING NOTES

Page 4 Write the five themes on the chalkboard. Help students pronounce the themes. Have students describe what they see in the photograph on page 4. Have students look at the photograph as you read the text aloud. Then read the question to students. Discuss their answers. Point out that every place on Earth has its own specific location.

Page 5 Read the text at the top of page 5 to students. Have students look at the photograph of the city. Ask: How is this city like your city? How is it different? Explain that place tells what the location is like. Does it have mountains? Does it get a lot of rain? Do people live in houses of stone and wood, or in tents on the desert? Point out that each place is different and special. Have students answer question 2.

◆ Read aloud the text about human/environment interaction. Have students look at the photograph and then answer question 3.

Page 6 Read the text on the top of page 6 to students as they study the photograph. Have students answer question 4. Discuss their answers.

◆ Read the text about regions to students. Discuss what they see in the photograph.

Page 7 Have students answer question 5. Then discuss what characteristics might make your area a region. Have students work the rest of the exercises on page 7. Point out to students that they will learn more about the five ways to study geography in special features called "Geography Themes Up Close" throughout *Maps•Globes•Graphs*.

EXTENSION ACTIVITIES

◆ Have students draw five pictures—one to represent each theme. You may wish to display the appropriate theme drawings at the chalkboard or on a bulletin board each time you study one of the geography theme features in the text.

Pictures

OBJECTIVES

Student will
◆ compare a photo and a drawing
◆ distinguish a drawing from a photo
◆ match objects in a drawing with objects in a photo

MATERIALS NEEDED

camera
photos and drawings
large photo of something with a simple shape
Blackline Master T21
Transparency 1
magazines

VOCABULARY

photo   drawing

INTRODUCING THE SKILL

◆ Have students look at the cover of the book and decide which images are photos and which are drawings. All the cover images appear within the book and are listed in the credits as photographs or illustrations.
◆ Point out that photos are taken with a camera. Bring in a camera to show the class, and if possible, take a photo of the entire class. Divide the class into small groups. Have several photos and drawings selected to show each group. Have students answer questions orally about details in the photos and drawings. Point out and discuss similarities and differences between the photos and drawings.
◆ Show students a large photo, such as one found on a calendar, of something with a simple shape, such as a hot-air balloon, a piece of fruit, a toy, a car, or a kite. Ask students to make a drawing of the photo and match the colors they see in the photo.
◆ Distribute copies of the scarecrow blackline on page T21 to students. Have students follow your directions about what colors to use to complete the picture.

TEACHING NOTES

Page 8   Use Transparency 1 to introduce the concepts on this page.
Pages 8 and 9   Ask students if they can find things in the photo that are not in the drawings. As students name items, have them underline those items on the photo. Next, ask how the photo and drawings are different (*the drawings are not the same size as the photo; the drawings only show a small part of what is in the photo; and the photo is a picture of a real place that was taken by a person with a camera, but the drawings are pictures of a real place that were made by an artist*).

Page 10   Discuss specific items in the drawing and have students circle those items as you name them. Next, have students discuss similarities and differences between this drawing and the photo on page 8.
Page 11   Direct students to draw a red chimney on the roof of the house. Next, ask students to draw a blue car on the street. You may wish to have students add other items to the picture.
Page 12   Initiate a class discussion to have students tell how the school on page 12 is different from their school. You might ask students if their school is made out of brick, whether students ride to and from school on school buses, if their school has two stories (or floors), etc. Next, ask students to name things that they see in the photo that are not in the drawing.
Page 13   If students need additional practice comparing a photo to a drawing, have them point out things that are found in the photo but not found in the drawing (*the house is made of bricks, red flowers are near the door, a light is above the door, and a plant is in the center window*).

EXTENSION ACTIVITIES

◆ Have students find and cut out photos of various objects in magazines and draw those objects. Then divide the class into small groups. Have students shuffle the photos and drawings and play a game in which they find the matching pairs.
◆ Have students draw or cut out pictures from magazines to create a worksheet that shows absurdities, such as an elephant walking around in a house. On the front of the worksheet, have students write, "What's wrong with this picture?" On the back of the worksheet, have them write the number of absurdities that can be found in the picture they have created. Then ask students to trade worksheets with a partner and identify the absurdities in each other's pictures.
◆ Take a photo of each student in the classroom. Give students their photo, and have them make a drawing of themselves and color it to match the photo. Display the drawings and photos on a bulletin board.

AT HOME ACTIVITY

◆ Ask students to have a family member help them find a photo of something they would like to draw. The photo could be one that someone in the family has taken or one found in a book, magazine, or newspaper. Ask students to make a drawing of the photo and bring both items to share with the class.

OBJECTIVES

Students will

◆ match names with pictures of ways to move people and goods

◆ name additional ways to move people and goods

◆ analyze an illustration and identify ways that ideas are communicated

MATERIALS NEEDED

magazines and newspapers
Blackline Master T22

VOCABULARY

movement

INTRODUCING THE SKILL

◆ Make a chart on the chalkboard entitled *Movement*. Under the title write the following headings: *People, Goods, Ideas*. Ask students to brainstorm ways people get from one place to another. Write their answers under the heading *People*. Next, ask students to brainstorm ways goods get from place to place. Write their answers under the heading *Goods*. Finally, ask students to brainstorm ways ideas get from place to place. This concept may be difficult for students to understand at first, so you may want to prompt them with questions to elicit the correct answers. Ask: How do you find out what kind of weather there will be tomorrow? How do you find out what is happening in your neighborhood? Write their answers under the heading *Ideas*. Tell students that in this feature they will learn about the movement of people, goods, and ideas.

TEACHING NOTES

Page 14 Read the introductory paragraph to students. Then have them draw a line to match each word with its picture. Then have students answer question 2.

◆ Ask students to fold a piece of paper in half. Then have them fold the paper in half again so that there are four squares. Ask them to unfold the paper and draw four pictures of things that they (or someone they know) use to move themselves and goods from place to place besides those pictured on this page. Have them write the name of each object under its picture. (*Pictures might include: bicycles, wagons, rollerblades, skis, cars, snowmobiles, small boats, buses, and so on*)

◆ Ask students: How do you get to school? How do your parents get to work? How does your family get to stores? How do you and your family get to places to have fun?

Page 15 Read aloud the introductory paragraph. Then read question 3 to students. Have students look at the drawing and circle the ways that we get ideas. When they finish, discuss their answers. Ask: How do each of these things move ideas? What are other ways to get ideas?

EXTENSION ACTIVITIES

◆ Have students work in small groups to list things that come into their neighborhoods from other places.

◆ Discuss how highways, railways, and airports tie people together.

◆ Take a survey to determine the ways students and teachers travel to and from school. (*Answers may include walking, rollerblading, bicycling, riding in a car, riding in a bus, and so on.*) Work with students to construct a graph or chart showing the results of the survey. Then discuss what the graph or chart shows. Display the graph or chart in the classroom.

◆ Have students evaluate the best way of moving the following goods and people from place to place: large rocks from a quarry to a building site; food grown on farms to a store; milk from a dairy farm to the factory that puts it in milk cartons; a hockey team that is going to play another team far away; drinking water from a lake to a town.

◆ Have students write a message to a friend and mail it. Have students write an e-mail message to another friend. Discuss which method of sending a message is faster. Discuss why this is so.

◆ Have students create another chart like the one created for the introductory skill, using the same title and headings. Give students copies of the blackline master of transportation symbols on page T22 and some magazines. Ask students to cut out the transportation symbols on page T22 and magazine pictures of ways that people, goods, and ideas move. You may wish to have students color the symbols from the blackline master. Then have students tape or glue the symbols and pictures in the correct place on the chart.

AT HOME ACTIVITY

◆ Have students work with family members to discuss the routes they follow from home to school. If possible, have family members work with students to draw the route. Students and family members might also discuss the routes they take to get from home to other places in the neighborhood.

OBJECTIVES

Students will
◆ compare ground view and aerial view photos
◆ match an aerial view photo with an aerial view drawing
◆ locate and match objects in a drawing with objects in a photo

MATERIALS NEEDED

aerial view photos or drawings
apples
field trip to scenic overlook, mountain or hill, top of building, etc.
Transparency 2
Blackline Master T22
magazines
construction paper

VOCABULARY

photo   drawing

INTRODUCING THE SKILL

◆ Show students aerial view photos or drawings and discuss the difference between ground level and aerial points of view. Have students identify objects in the aerial views. Point out that color is often helpful in recognizing objects.
◆ Have students practice looking at things from different points of view. Give each student an apple. Have them observe the apple from eye-level, from above, and from below. Have students describe what they see. Have them compare and contrast the different perspectives. Then let students eat their apple as a treat.
◆ Take students on a field trip to a high point in the community, such as a scenic overlook, mountain or hill, top of a building, elevated walkway, etc. Have students record their observations, noting what they saw from the high point and what they saw at a lower level.

TEACHING NOTES

Page 16 Use Transparency 2 to introduce the concepts on this page.
Pages 16 and 17 Ask students to circle the swimming pool in both photographs. Ask them why the pool on page 17 looks larger. Lead students to conclude that the pool on page 17 looks larger because the person taking the photo was looking down from above the playground, so more of the pool can be seen. The person taking the photo on page 16 was standing on the ground, so only part of the pool can be seen. Then have students explain how the position of the person

taking the photographs affects the size of the tire swing as it is shown on pages 16 and 17.
Page 18 Before students color the drawing have them draw themselves in the area of the drawing that they would most like to play. Encourage volunteers to share their drawings with the rest of the class.
Page 19 Have students draw a picture of their own bedroom or a picture of what their ideal or "dream" bedroom would look like. Encourage students to label items included in their bedroom.
Page 20 Give students extra practice finding things in a picture by having them count the people they see in the picture (*14*), the street lights (*6*), and windows that can be seen on the bus (*8*). Next, direct students to find the woman in the green dress with the yellow hat and draw a circle around her. Have them do the same to the picture of the man in the blue sweater and gray pants. Finally, have students find the City Bank building and mark an *X* on it.
Page 21 Have students find a simple photo in a magazine and make a drawing of that item, matching the colors in the photo.

EXTENSION ACTIVITIES

◆ Take students outside to the school playground or a nearby playground. Have them name every thing they can see at the playground. Make a list of all items mentioned and copy the list onto chart paper or the chalkboard upon returning to the classroom. Direct students to make a drawing of the playground using the items in the list as a reference. Display the drawings on a bulletin board.
◆ Divide the class into small groups. Give each group a copy of the blackline on page T22 and three sheets of construction paper. Have students glue the drawings of the car, boat, airplane, horse, bicycle, train, bus, van, pickup truck, and multi-wheeled truck and glue them the top of the construction paper, one per sheet. Have them make transportation posters by cutting out and gluing magazine pictures of cars, boats, airplanes, horses, etc., on the appropriate poster. Have the class discuss which pictures on the finished posters are drawings and which ones are photos. Also discuss which point of view is shown in each picture: eye level, from above, or from below.

AT HOME ACTIVITY

◆ Have students work with a family member to choose an item at home and make two drawings of the item. The first drawing should be looking down from above, and the second drawing should be an eye-level view. Encourage volunteers to share their drawings with the class.

OBJECTIVES

Students will
◆ match shapes and colors on a map with features in a photo
◆ locate objects on a map
◆ determine exact location

MATERIALS NEEDED

various maps
Blackline Masters T22 and T28
Transparency 3
aerial view photos

VOCABULARY

photo   map

INTRODUCING THE SKILL

◆ Have students bring maps from home for a map show-and-tell. Ask students questions such as "What can you recognize on the maps? How are the maps alike? How are they different?" Have students brainstorm a list of different uses for the maps. Display the various maps on a bulletin board.
◆ Provide students with copies of the blackline map of the United States on page T28. Have students color the map so states that touch each other are not the same color.
◆ Have students draw a simple map of the area around the school or around their home. Make copies of the blackline symbols on the left side of page T22 for students to cut out and use on their map.

TEACHING NOTES

Page 22   Use Transparency 3 to introduce the concepts on this page.
Pages 22 and 23   Make a list with students of the things that are shown in the photo but not shown on the map (*cars, the railroad crossing symbol on the street, railroad tracks, street lights, water, mailboxes, and various items on lawns*). Ask students why they think all those things would not be included on the map. (*Accept any reasonable explanations.*) Finally, have students circle the house in which they would like to live. Call on volunteers to tell the class why they chose a particular house.
Page 24   Ask students where they think the photographer was when the photo on page 24 was taken (*in an airplane or helicopter*). Next, ask students what the blue rectangle on the photo is (*a swimming pool*). Ask students to compare and contrast the photo and the drawing.
Page 26   Have students select one pet on the map that they would most like to own. Direct students to circle that animal and write one sentence in the space to the right of the directions to explain why

they chose that animal. Make a chart on the chalkboard listing a category for the dog, fish, turtles, orange lizard, and green lizard. Have students come to the chalkboard and make a mark by the name of the animal they chose. Discuss the completed chart with the class.
Page 27   If students need extra practice matching shapes and colors on a map with features in a photo, give clues using colors to describe a certain feature on the map, and have students circle that on the map. Next, describe a feature on the map, and have students circle that feature on the photo.

EXTENSION ACTIVITIES

◆ Bring in several aerial-view photos similar to the ones used in this chapter. Divide the class into small groups, and give each group one of the photos and a large sheet of paper. Direct each group to work cooperatively to create a map of the area shown in the photo. Instruct them to color the map to match the photo. Invite each group to share their map with the class before displaying the photos and maps in the classroom.
◆ Divide the class into cooperative learning groups. Tell students that they are going to make a map of an imaginary town. Have students brainstorm a list of features, such as houses, schools, stores, fire stations, etc., that they might want to include on their town map. Then provide each group with a large sheet of butcher paper so they can create a section of the town. After the groups have completed their section, tape the sections together to make a large wall map of the imaginary town.
◆ Divide the class into groups. Tell students they will be making a map of the school, hall, or wing. A tour of the school may be helpful for students. Have students discuss the various areas they will include on their maps, such as the principal's office, nurse's office, cafeteria, library, gym, playground, etc. Provide a piece of butcher paper to each group. Have each group draw a map of part of the school. Be sure each student in the group contributes something to the map. Then have students label each different area or classroom. Hang the completed maps in the hallway for others to enjoy.

AT HOME ACTIVITY

◆ Encourage students to ask a family member to help them make a simple map of their home or a room in their home. Ask them to color their maps, matching the items on the map with the real items in their home. Invite volunteers to share their maps with the rest of the class.

Geography Themes Up Close

OBJECTIVES

Students will
◆ match names and pictures of places
◆ name places
◆ identify the features of a place using a map

MATERIALS NEEDED

One Morning in Maine or *Make Way for Ducklings*
   by Robert McCloskey, *Charlotte's Web* by
   E. B. White, or *The Snowy Day* by Ezra Jacks Keats
pictures of neighborhoods
sand table, modeling clay, blocks, or cardboard

VOCABULARY

place

INTRODUCING THE SKILL

◆ Have students draw a picture of their classroom. Tell them to pretend they are sitting on the ceiling looking down at the classroom and to draw what they see. Have them indicate where they sit with an *X*. Give students about five minutes to complete their drawings. When finished, have students share their drawings. Then say, "Our classroom is a place. What things make up our classroom?" Students should indicate things such as the chalkboards, desks, books, and so forth. Point out that in this feature, they will learn more about the things that make places different from one another.

TEACHING NOTES

Page 28   Read and discuss with students the introductory sentences on this page. Then have students look at the words and pictures in question 1. Tell students that each word is a name of a place and each picture is a picture of the place. Then have students draw a line to match each place name with its correct picture. Once they are finished, call on volunteers to share their answers. Then ask students what features of each picture indicates what kind of place it is. Next, create a Venn diagram on the chalkboard to compare and contrast the features of the city with the features of the farm. Repeat this activity with all the places pictured on this page.
◆ Have students look at the places shown on pages 17, 20, 22, and 27. Ask: How are these places different from one another? (*Answers will vary, but should contrast features of the places.*)
Page 29   Read the introductory sentences on this page. Have students look at the map of Ling's neighborhood. Have students follow the directions and answer questions 3–5. Point out that Ling's neighborhood has features which make it unique from any other place. Ask: How is Ling's

neighborhood different from your neighborhood? Ask students to identify features in their neighborhoods.
◆ Discuss with students the fact that their home is different from any other place. Tell them that even if the outside of their house looks like other homes, it is different because of the way people decorate the inside with paint, wallpaper, and furniture. Tell them that the house is different from other homes because the people who live in the homes are different.
◆ Take students for a walk in the neighborhood around the school. Tell students to observe the things that make up the neighborhood. When students returns to the classroom, make a map of the school neighborhood. Include the following on the map: streets, buildings, parks, and any other features students can remember. If it is not possible to walk through the neighborhood, take a walk through the school building and then make a map of the school showing its unique features.

EXTENSION ACTIVITIES

◆ Provide students with pictures of several neighborhoods. Ask students to identify the features in each neighborhood. Ask students to share their findings with the class.
◆ Have students make a model of their neighborhood using a sand table, modeling clay, blocks, or cardboard. Ask students to describe their model to the class.
◆ Tell students that the kind of weather a place has helps tell what the place is like. Ask students to describe what the weather is like today where they live.
◆ Have students pretend to be television reporters who are visiting the community. Their job is to describe the community to the television viewers. Students should tell viewers about the important features of the community.
◆ Read story books to students that describe imaginary and real places. You might read books such as *One Morning in Maine* by Robert McCloskey, *Make Way for Ducklings* by Robert McCloskey, *Charlotte's Web* by E. B. White, or *The Snowy Day* by Ezra Jacks Keats. Then ask students to identify the features of the places described in each story.

AT HOME ACTIVITY

◆ Have students work with family members to make a visual survey of their neighborhood or community. Students can draw pictures or take photographs of special features in their neighborhood or community. Then have them use the drawings or photographs to create a picture book about their neighborhood or community.

OBJECTIVES
Students will
◆ identify and locate top, bottom, right, and left
◆ determine exact location using top, bottom, right, and left

MATERIALS NEEDED
Transparency 4
colored tape
butcher paper
simple mazes or game boards (laminated)
Blackline Masters T23, T24, T25
number cube, game markers or tokens

VOCABULARY
top   right
bottom   left

INTRODUCING THE SKILL
◆ Have students practice locating top, bottom, right, and left on items in the classroom such as their desks, chairs, the chalkboard, pictures, and books. Have students make labels for top, bottom, right, and left, using construction paper. Have them tape these labels to their desk tops, lockers, etc. Direct students to label their papers for other daily assignments with *top*, *bottom*, *right*, and *left*.
◆ Give students a sheet of drawing paper. Have students label their paper with the words with *top*, *bottom*, *right*, and *left*. Now direct students to draw and color simple shapes in each of the four directions on their paper. For example, "Draw three red hearts at the top of your paper. Draw two green squares at the bottom of your paper. Draw four orange circles on the right side of your paper. Draw one blue diamond on the left side of your paper."

TEACHING NOTES
Page 30   Use Transparency 4 to introduce the concepts on this page.
Pages 30 and 31   Place colored tape on the floor to divide the classroom into sections. Then divide the class into groups according to the section in which students' desks are located. Give a large sheet of butcher paper to each group. Have the groups work cooperatively to create a map of their section of the classroom. Be sure each student's desk is drawn on the map. Have students label their desk on the map with their name. After students have completed making a map of their section of the classroom, tape the pieces of butcher paper together to form one large map of the classroom. Then have students label the four sides of the map using pages 30 and 31 as models. Display the map on a wall or in the hallway for others to enjoy.

Page 32   To provide extra practice in finding items at the *top*, *bottom*, *right*, and *left* of a drawing, ask students to tell on which side of the picture on page 32 they would look to find the tallest building (*right*). Ask where they would look to find the airplane (*top*), to find the streetlight (*left*), and to find the fire hydrant (*bottom*).
Pages 34 and 35   Make several simple mazes or game boards for students. Make *top*, *bottom*, *right*, and *left* labels for each game board. Use directions and arrows or simple pictures similar to those on page 34. Laminate the game boards or cover them with transparent contact paper so that they can be reused. Allow students to use overhead transparency markers to color the arrows or pictures. The game boards can be wiped clean with a damp paper towel.

EXTENSION ACTIVITIES
◆ Divide the class into groups. Have each group make a kite with the four points labeled *top*, *bottom*, *right*, and *left*. The kites can be made out of thin dowels or strips of balsa wood covered with paper. Have students make a tail for their kite out of strips of fabric. Have them attach some kite string. Then take the class outside on a windy day to fly the kites.
◆ Divide the class into pairs of students. Give each pair a copy of the game board blacklines on pages T24 and T25, a number cube, and two tokens. Have students color their game board and make up a game that practices using top, bottom, right, and left. Allow students time to play the game they have made up so they can evaluate it. Then have each pair of students explain to the class the rules of the game they created.
◆ Give each student a copy of the classroom blackline on page T23. Have students color and cut out the symbol labels and the direction labels on the bottom of page T23. Then direct students to paste the labels on the picture of the classroom. For example, you might say: "Paste the flag label near the top." Or, "Paste the table on the left side of the room." Continue directing students until all the labels have been placed on the picture. Then have pairs of students ask each other to describe the location of certain items on the picture.

AT HOME ACTIVITY
◆ Have students ask a family member to help them make a list of items in their home that have four sides, such as a refrigerator, bed, TV, etc. Encourage students to share their lists with the class.

OBJECTIVES

Students will

◆ locate south, east, and west in relation to north

◆ determine exact location using direction

◆ recognize *N, S, E,* and *W* as abbreviations for north, south, east, and west

MATERIALS NEEDED

Blackline Masters T21, T25, T26–T27
Transparency 5
compass
colored outdoor chalk
small playing pieces or markers

VOCABULARY

north   east
south   west

INTRODUCING THE SKILL

◆ Take students outside on a sunny day at noon and have them face their shadows. They will be facing north. South will be behind them. East will be to their right, and west will be to their left. Have students locate landmarks in each direction.

◆ Have copies of the scarecrow on page T21 ready for students to color, cut out, and paste in the center of a large sheet of paper. (*To make the scarecrow stand up, mount it on poster board with tabs added to its feet.*) Direct students to label the paper with an *N* at the top, *S* at the bottom, *E* on the right, and *W* on the left. Then have students illustrate the landmarks they saw in each direction during the activity above.

TEACHING NOTES

Page 36   Take students outside to a sidewalk or paved area on the playground. Using a compass and several different colors of chalk, draw the outline for two or three compass roses similar to the one on page 36. Divide the class into groups. Have students color each compass rose with the chalk and label the four cardinal directions with *N, S, E,* and *W.* Have students take turns standing in the center of their compass rose while you call out a direction. Have the student in each compass rose name an object in that direction.

Page 37   Use Transparency 5 to introduce the concepts on this page. Ask students which direction the farmer is facing (*north*). Ask students if they can find any other things in the north part of the farm besides the barn (*trees and the field*). Have students draw a line from the farmer's right hand to the object on the farm that he is pointing to (*haystack*), and direct them to circle it. Next, have

students draw a line from the farmer's left hand to the object he is pointing to (*truck*), and have them make an *X* on it. Now ask which direction the farmer would be facing if he turned around (*south*).

Page 38   If students have difficulty with cardinal directions, give them additional practice before progressing to page 39. Provide students with copies of the toy store and labels blacklines on pages T26 and T27. Have students color and cut out the symbols and labels on page T27. Then direct students to paste the labels in the appropriate places in the toy store by using directional prompts. For example, say: "Paste the video games on the north side of the store." Continue until students have completed filling the toy store.

Page 39   Read and work through the first item with students. Ask them to place a finger on the word *start* at the flower gardens. Have them move their finger in the direction to get to the ducks. Have them draw an arrow showing this path. Ask students to name and circle the correct letter for the direction they moved. You may wish to work through additional items with students. Then have students identify other things that they would pass as they make a path through the park and tell which direction each thing is from the path.

Page 40   Have students name the directions they would go if they started at the popcorn stand and went in the reverse order to get back to the gate.

Page 41   Use a compass to determine direction and take the class to the school library. Starting at the door, select items such as the globe, card catalog, etc., and have students determine which direction they would go to get from one item to another.

EXTENSION ACTIVITIES

◆ Provide students with copies of the compass rose blackline on page T25. Have them follow the directions to make the compass rose game. The spinner can be used to play the following game.

◆ Have students use the map on pages 60 and 61 as a game board. They will need small playing pieces or markers. Each player places a marker on the state of Kansas. Students take turns with the game spinner and move their markers to the next state in the direction the spinner indicates. The first student to reach a large body of water wins the game.

AT HOME ACTIVITY

◆ Have students draw a picture of the outside of their home. Then encourage them to have a family member help them determine which direction their home faces and label the drawing with *N, S, E,* and *W.*

Geography Themes Up Close

OBJECTIVES

Students will
◆ identify regions on maps
◆ determine the features used to organize regions

MATERIALS NEEDED

magazines and newspapers
map of the local community

VOCABULARY

regions

INTRODUCING THE SKILL

◆ Have students look at the picture on page 33 in *Maps•Globes•Graphs*. Point out to students that this picture shows a region. The region it shows is a zoo. Ask: What will you find in a zoo? (*animals*) Explain that all zoos are alike because they all have animals. Ask students to explain how a zoo would be different from a mall. (*Zoos are places where people go to see animals. Malls are places where people go to buy goods.*) Point out that all malls are alike because they all have stores for shopping. Explain that in this feature they will learn about other places that are regions because they are alike.

TEACHING NOTES

Page 42   Read and discuss with students the introductory sentences at the top of page 42. Ask: How are all mountain regions alike? (*They all have mountains. Mountains are high places. It snows in mountains. There are trees and animals in mountains.*) Point out that the shape of the land is one way that places in a region are alike. Next, read the second group of sentences to the students. Point out that the science table is a region because everything on the table has something to do with science.
◆ Have students complete items 1–3. When they are finished, discuss with students how student desks make up a region, the computers are a region, and the reading area is a region. Ask them to describe the feature used to organize each region. Then have students organize their own classroom into regions. Ask them to describe the features used to organize each region.
Page 43   Have students look at the map. Tell students that this map shows the community of Jollyville. Have students locate the directional arrows on the map. Then have them complete item 4. Discuss the answers when all students have finished. Ask students to describe the feature that is alike, or common, in each region. (*forest region: trees is the common feature; house region, houses; store region: stores; park region: playground and equipment*) Finally, have students draw a region in the empty space in the center of the map. Call on volunteers to name their region and explain the common feature of the region.
◆ Point out to students that their home is a region. The block they live on is a region. The neighborhood they live in is a region. And the community they live in is a region. Explain that wherever a person lives, they are part of many regions all at the same time. Students can even organize their bedroom into regions. One region could be the beds where people sleep. Another region could be the area where toys are kept. A third region could be the area where books are kept. A fourth region could be the closet or the chest of drawers where clothes are kept.
◆ Have students look at the maps on pages 34, 35, and 37. Ask them to name the region that each map shows. (*Page 34 shows a garden; page 35 shows a living room; page 37 shows a farm*) Ask: How can the region shown on page 37 be furthered divided into regions on the farm? (*There is a crop region; barn region; cow pen region, and haystack.*)

EXTENSION ACTIVITIES

◆ Have students find pictures of neighborhoods or communities in magazines and newspapers. Have them draw circles around regions they see in each picture. Have students describe the regions in their pictures.
◆ Have students identify regions in their neighborhood. Ask them to describe the common feature of each region.
◆ Have students use a map of the local community to find all the areas where people live. Have them color these areas the same color. Then have them find areas where there are stores. Have them color these areas the same color. Then have them find areas where there are parks. Have them color these areas the same color. Finally, have students analyze the map to discover the way their community is organized by regions.

AT HOME ACTIVITY

◆ Have students work with family members to draw a picture of their home. Ask them to show the regions in their home.

OBJECTIVES

Students will
- match map key symbols with symbols on a map
- add symbols to a map
- determine relative location using direction
- distinguish a symbol from a photo

MATERIALS NEEDED

Transparencies 6 and 7
Blackline Masters T22, T28, T29
butcher paper
materials to make a board game: posterboard, paints, crayons, or markers, symbol or flash cards, dice, game markers

VOCABULARY

symbol   map key

INTRODUCING THE SKILL

- Have students identify symbols they use at school (+, –, =, $, and ¢ for add, subtract, equals, dollars, and cents). List familiar symbols such as color on traffic lights, various road signs, and holiday symbols like pumpkins, turkeys, and hearts. Now have students make up symbols for common items.
- Have students practice identifying symbols on map keys using maps found in the classroom, library, or in basal textbooks. Ask for volunteers to find matching symbols on the maps.
- Using chart paper or posterboard, make a chart or graph that the entire class can fill in with a symbol for their eye or shoe color. Have each student draw and color a pair of eyes or shoes above the label of their own eye or shoe color. Discuss the chart and use of symbols.

TEACHING NOTES

Pages 44 and 45 Use Transparencies 6 and 7 to introduce the concepts on this page. Explain to students that symbols are often used on maps to stand for something that is real. Discuss how a map key unlocks a map. Have students read the label next to each symbol on the map key on page 45. Then have them draw a line to connect each symbol in the map key to its matching symbol on the map.
Pages 46 and 47 Take students on a walk through the neighborhood surrounding your school. Direct students to find at least three things for which they could draw a symbol. Upon returning to class, have students draw, color, and cut out their symbols. Draw a simple picture or symbol of the school in the center of a large sheet of butcher paper. Create a map of the neighborhood by pasting students' symbols around the school. Students can then add

streets, cars, buses, etc., to the map. Display the map on a bulletin board or in the hallway.
Page 48 Have students complete the page. Then direct students to find the school on the map. Have them draw a line and tell you which direction they would be going from the school to the large house (*west*). Now have students draw a line and tell which direction they would be going from the large house to the two trees that have not been colored (*south*). Direct them to color the trees orange. Next, have students draw a line and tell which direction they would be going from the trees to the store (*east*) and their from the store to the factory (*north*).

EXTENSION ACTIVITIES

- Give students copies of the blackline map of the United States on page T28. Ask students to color one state in each section (*north, south, east, west*) of the country that they would like to visit. Then have students pretend to take a trip to the states they have colored. Ask them to write a story about their trip.
- Have copies of the blackline on page T22 available for students to use. Have students draw maps of their classroom, playground, or neighborhood. Students can draw their own symbols or use the symbols from page T22 for a map key.
- Divide the class into groups. Help each group design and create a Monopoly-like game board where students can create their own symbols in each of the squares. Some symbols can be for bad luck, where the player is sent backward, and others can be for good luck, where the player is sent ahead or gets an extra turn. Each time players pass start, they earn a symbol card (*perhaps a card with a sticker or happy face on it*). Reading or math flash cards can be used to play this game. If students read the word and solve the math problem correctly, they get to roll the dice and move on the game board. The player with the most symbol cards at the end of the game wins.
- Divide the class into cooperative learning groups. Provide each group with a copy of the blackline map of the world on page T29. Help students do research to find out what interesting animals, plants, or natural features are found on each continent. Have students create symbols to present the information on their map. Be sure they add a map key to the map so their symbols can be understood. Ask each group to explain the information shown on their map.

AT HOME ACTIVITY

- Invite students to have a family member help them create symbols for three items in their home.

Geography Themes Up Close

OBJECTIVES

Students will

◆ identify ways that people depend on the environment
◆ understand and illustrate ways people change the land
◆ describe ways people change the land

MATERIALS NEEDED

The Little Engine that Could retold by Watty Piper
field trips to environments, such as greenhouses, indoor swimming pools, or indoor sports stadiums
magazines

VOCABULARY

human/environment interaction

INTRODUCING THE SKILL

◆ Have students brainstorm ways that the following weather might affect them: rain, snow, hot temperatures, cold temperatures, lightning, heavy winds. Encourage students to talk about the kinds of clothing they would wear, activities they could or couldn't do, and other ways the weather might affect them. Then tell students that in this feature they will learn more about how people live in and with the world around them.

TEACHING NOTES

Page 50   Read and discuss with students the introductory paragraph on page 50. Ask students if they can name other examples of how people use the land. Then have students look at the pictures and sentences on the page. Ask students to draw a line to match each picture with the sentence that tells about it. Discuss the answers with students.
◆ Point out that each picture shows how people's lives are influenced by where they live. Emphasize that the environment of a place helps decide what people will wear, what kinds of jobs people can do, and how people can have fun. You might have pictures of various environments available for students to view. Ask them to give examples of the kinds of clothing, the jobs, and the kinds of recreation that would be available or suited to each environment pictured.
◆ Have students describe how their environment influences what they wear, the kinds of jobs people in their area have, and how people have fun.
Page 51   Read the introductory sentences aloud. Then direct students to complete question 2. Call on volunteers to share their drawings. Then have students answer question 3. Discuss their answers.
◆ Have students look at the picture on page 44. Ask: How have people changed the land in this

photo? What was the land like before it was changed?
◆ Have photos or magazine pictures available to show students positive and negative results of people having changed the land. Some negative examples might include the results of different kinds of pollution, the destruction of rain forests or animal habitats, etc. Some positive examples could include cleaning a river or lake (the story of Lake Erie), beach cleanups, reforestation efforts of various groups (Arbor Day activities), and establishing refuges and preserves to protect animals and certain ecosystems such as marshes or wetlands.

EXTENSION ACTIVITIES

◆ Work with students to make a chart showing ways all people depend on the air, water, and land. The title of the chart could be *How People Use Air, Water, and Land*. The headings in the chart should be *Air, Water, Land*. Have students brainstorm ways that people depend on air, water, and land. Write their response on the chart. Then discuss with students what happens when air, water, and land are polluted by people.
◆ Read students books that focus on the environment and how it affects people. For example, you might read, *The Little Engine that Could* retold by Watty Piper. Discuss how the mountain affected the people, the toys, and the trains.
◆ Have students make a list of people that they depend upon to meet their needs and wants, within and outside the home.
◆ Arrange field trips to places where people create environments, such as greenhouses, indoor swimming pools, or indoor sports stadiums. Have workers at these places answer questions about the problems involved in creating such environments.
◆ Have students find pictures in magazines showing tools in schools and in homes that make it easier for people to use the environment. For example, a shovel makes it easier to dig holes in the soil in order to plant trees and bushes.
◆ Encourage students to clean the litter around the school. Discuss with students the effects of cleaning up litter in their neighborhoods.
◆ Discuss with students the importance of recycling glass, plastic, newspapers, aluminum, and other materials.

AT HOME ACTIVITY

◆ Have students work with family members to observe and describe ways they are influenced by the environment and how they change the environment. Have students share their descriptions with the class.

OBJECTIVES

Students will
◆ use a map key to color a globe
◆ distinguish land from water on a globe
◆ locate the United States, Canada, and Mexico on a globe
◆ locate countries and oceans using directions

MATERIALS NEEDED

globe
map of your state
Blackline Masters T22 and T29
large balloons
supplies to make papier-mâché
paints
Transparency 8
a small person drawn on heavy paper with tabs for both feet
tape
orange or grapefruit
marker
knife

VOCABULARY

globe	Atlantic Ocean
model	Pacific Ocean
North America	United States (U.S.)
South America	Mexico
Equator	Canada

INTRODUCING THE SKILL

◆ Show students a globe. Demonstrate how places, such as the United States, can be found on the globe. Discuss the colors used on the globe to show land and water. Identify the Atlantic Ocean, Pacific Ocean, North Pole, South Pole, and Equator.

◆ Divide the class into groups. Distribute copies of the blackline master on page T22 to students. Have them use the cut-out transportation symbols (*car, boat, airplane, etc.*) to take imaginary trips between places on a globe. Ask students to name the direction they are traveling. Provide students with copies of the blackline map of the world on page T29 to trace their route.

◆ Have students blow up large balloons and cover them with papier-mâché. After the papier-mâché has dried, have students paint the oceans and continents to make a globe. Hang the globes from the ceiling.

TEACHING NOTES

Page 52 Show students a globe with continents, countries, etc., labeled on it and have them compare and contrast the globe with the photo of Earth on page 52. First ask how they are the same. (*They both show that Earth is round and made up of water and land.*) Then ask how they are different. (*The globe uses labels and is shown in colors that are different from the real Earth.*) To give students an easy way to visualize their location on Earth, draw a small person on heavy paper with tabs for both feet. Cut the person out and fold one tab forward and one tab back so that your person can stand up on a globe. Tape the person above your location on the globe.

Page 53 Use Transparency 8 to introduce the concepts on this page. Explain to students that they live on the continent of North America. Show them North America on a globe and them have them circle it on the map on page 53. Tell students that the map shows only two continents, North America and South America, but that there are five other continents. Point out the other five continents on the globe. Slowly spin the globe and ask students if they think Earth is mostly land or water. When students answer "water," ask them what those large bodies of water are called (*oceans*). Show students the Atlantic Ocean and the Pacific Ocean on the globe, and have them draw a line under those two labels on the map.

Page 54 Show students the Equator on a globe and have them locate it on the map on page 54. Have them circle the label. Explain that the Equator is an imaginary circle that divides Earth in half. Next, show students the North Pole and the South Pole on the globe. Explain that the poles are the very top and bottom places on Earth. To demonstrate these concepts, use an orange or grapefruit. Show students the stem and tell them this represents the North Pole. Turn the fruit over and show them the bottom, which represents the South Pole. Now draw a line around the center to show the Equator. Cut the fruit in half to show that the Equator divides Earth in half.

EXTENSION ACTIVITY

◆ Show students where Alaska and Hawaii are located in relation to the rest of the United States. Have volunteers use a map or globe to locate the following: Canada, Mexico, the United States, their own home state, the Atlantic Ocean, and the Pacific Ocean.

AT HOME ACTIVITY

◆ Give students a copy of the blackline master of the world on page T29 to take home. Encourage students to ask family members to help them mark the map to show which countries their ancestors came from. Invite volunteers to share their maps with the rest of the class.

Geography Themes Up Close

OBJECTIVES

Students will
◆ locate places relative to other places using a map
◆ locate places using reference systems
◆ draw the locations of places on maps

MATERIALS NEEDED

The Little House, by Virginia Lee Burton
large world map

VOCABULARY

location

INTRODUCING THE SKILL

◆ Recite the following nursery rhyme to students. *Jack and Jill went up the hill to fetch a pail of water. Jack fell down and broke his crown and Jill came tumbling after.* Ask students to name the direction words in the rhyme. (*Up and down*) Then ask students to think of other nursery rhymes that include direction words. For example, they may recite, *Hickory, Dickory, Dock; Little Boy Blue; Little Miss Muffet;* and *London Bridge is Falling Down.* Write the direction words and phrases on the chalkboard. Explain to students that in this feature they will learn more about using direction words to describe the locations of places.

TEACHING NOTES

Page 58 Read aloud the introductory paragraph on this page. Have students turn to the atlas map of the United States on pages 60 and 61 and find Iowa on the map. Ask them to name the other states around Iowa besides Illinois. Then have them locate other states on the map. Next, have students look at the map of the United States on page 58. Have them follow the directions and complete the exercises on page 58. Discuss their answers. You may wish to have students locate and label all the states on the map on page 58.

◆ Give students more experience with location. Use the atlas map of the United States on pages 60 and 61 and play the game, "I'm thinking of a state that is . . ." Call on students to be the "thinker." The "thinker" might have students mark the state in some other way, such as by putting an *X* in pencil on this state. Next, help students list all the states that are located along the Atlantic Ocean, along the Pacific Ocean, along the border with Canada, and along the border with Mexico. Use a world map to show students the exact locations of Alaska and Hawaii.

Page 59 Read the introductory sentences aloud to students. Allow students time to complete the items on this page. Call on volunteers to share their completed maps with the class.
◆ Have students add roads to the map. Ask them to explain where they put the roads and why they put them there.
◆ Have students describe the location of Ruben's house relative to other places on the map.

EXTENSION ACTIVITIES

◆ Have students practice describing the location of places. Have them describe the location of the school. First, determine the directions north, south, east, and west in the classroom. Then ask: "What is north of the school?" "What is south of the school?" "What is east of the school?" "What is west of the school?"
◆ Read books about places that emphasize their locations, such as *The Little House*, by Virginia Lee Burton. While reading the story to students, show them the pictures of the location of the little house. Emphasize that although, at first, the little house did not move, things around it changed. Discuss how these changes affected what the house was near or what was around it. Then discuss why the little house was moved and describe its new location.
◆ Tell or print the home addresses of students. Compare street numbers, street names, city names, and zip codes.
◆ Help students locate their community on a local map, a state map, a map of the United States, and a world map.
◆ Take a walk around the school's block. Discuss the locations and reasons for such things as street signs, streetlights, stop signs, stoplights, fire hydrants, and fences.
◆ Ask students to identify locations of places in the classroom and school that could be used for quiet activities and those that should be used for noisy activities.

AT HOME ACTIVITY

◆ Have students work with family members to practice learning and writing their home addresses. Have them draw a neighborhood map, similar to the one on page 48. The student's home should be in the middle of the map and they should draw places that are around their home. The map should include a map key and the four cardinal directions. Have students share their maps with the class.

Letter to Families

Date _____

Dear Family:

Throughout the school year, your child will be learning and practicing geography skills by using *Maps•Globes•Graphs, Level A*. In the seven chapters, your child will learn to identify the four sides (top, bottom, left, and right) and relate them to the four directions (north, south, east, west). Your child will compare maps or drawings to photos and will work with maps learning to read symbols, labels, and directions. He or she will learn that the globe is a model of Earth and will learn to relate the four directions to the globe.

You can help your child reinforce what we study by asking him or her to talk to you about what we are doing. You might ask your child to explain some of the pictures and maps in the book.

You can also help your child by engaging in the following activity at home to support and reinforce our study of these skills.

Find pictures in books or magazines and discuss them with your child. Help your child identify and understand what is shown in the picture. Name things in the picture and ask your child to point them out and tell you the colors of items in the picture. Then have your child tell where the item is in relation to something else in the picture, with north being at the top of the picture, south at the bottom, east to the right, and west to the left.

Thank you for your interest and support.

Sincerely,

_____

Fecha _____

Estimada familia:

A lo largo de este año escolar, su hijo o hija aprenderá y practicará destrezas de geografía usando el programa *Maps•Globes•Graphs, Level A*. En los siete capítulos, su hijo o hija aprenderá a identificar los cuatro lados (encima, fondo, izquierda, derecha) y relatarlos a los cuatro direcciones (norte, sur, oeste, este). Su hijo o hija va a comparar mapas o dibujos a fotos y trabajará con mapas para aprender a leer símbolos, rótulos y direcciones. Él o ella aprenderá que el globo es un modelo de la tierra y aprenderá a relatar los cuatro direcciones al globo.

Usted puede ayudar a reforzar lo que estudiamos si pide que él o ella le cuente lo que hacemos en la clase. Quizás puede pedir que le explique algo de las fotos y los mapas en el libro.

También puede ayudarle con la siguiente actividad para reforzar las destrezas que estudiamos.

Encuentren fotos en libros o revistas y discútalas con su hijo o hija. Ayudele a identificar y comprender lo que se muestra en la foto. Nombren objetos en las fotos y pídale que los toque y que le diga los colores de los objectos en la foto. Su hijo o hija puede decirle donde está el objeto relatada a otra cosa en la foto. Norte está para arriba, sur al fondo, este a la derecha y oeste a la izquierda.

Gracias por su interés y apoyo.

Sinceramente,

_____

Name_____

Name _____

house
tree
lake
playground
swimming pool
school
store

Name_____

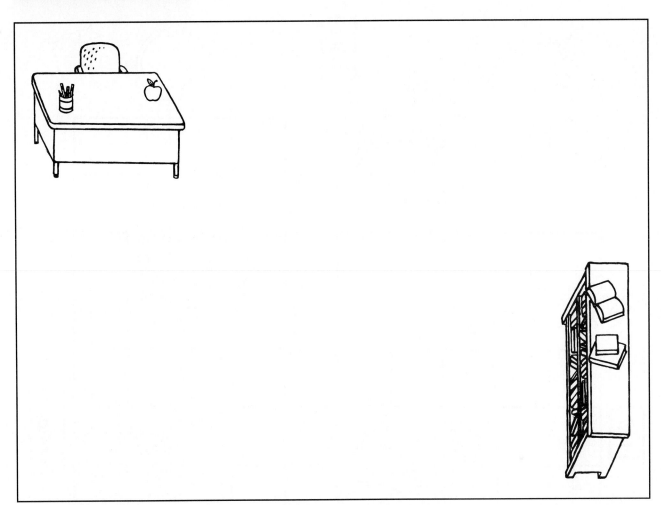

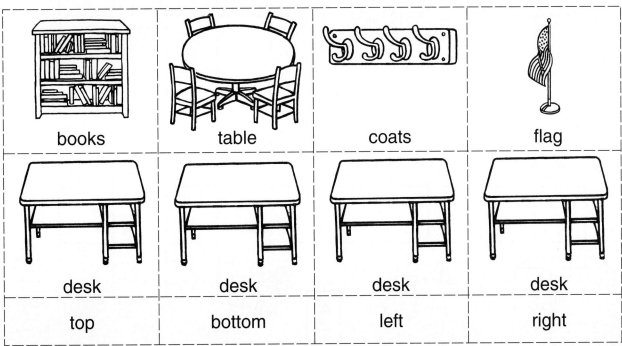

books	table	coats	flag
desk	desk	desk	desk
top	bottom	left	right

Name _____

AMUSEMENT PARK GAME BOARD

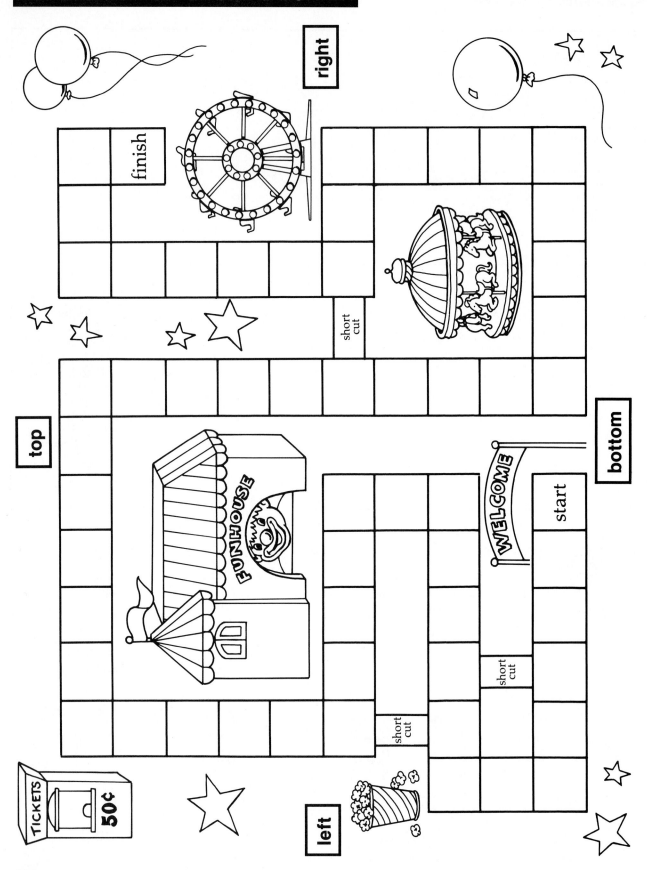

finish

right

short cut

top

bottom

FUNHOUSE

WELCOME

start

short cut

short cut

TICKETS 50¢

left

Name _____

COMPASS ROSE GAME SPINNER

| 1 | 2 | 3 | 4 |
| red | green | blue | orange |

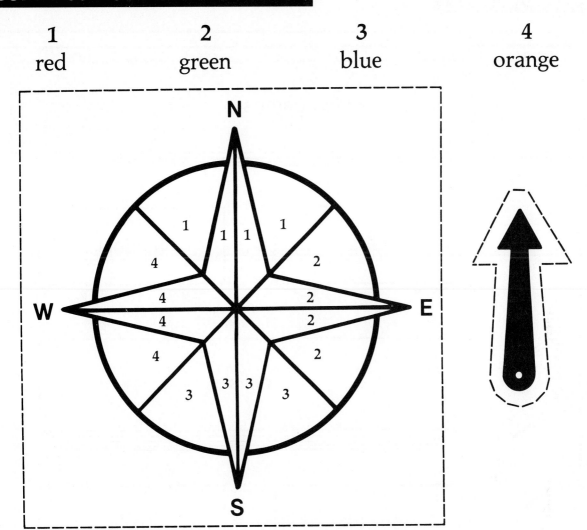

Directions for Making Game Spinner

Color compass rose by number. Cut out and mount on a piece of cardboard. Cut out and mount the black spinner arrow on a piece of heavy paper. Attach the arrow to the compass rose with a brass fastener.

| North | South |
| East | West |

Name_____

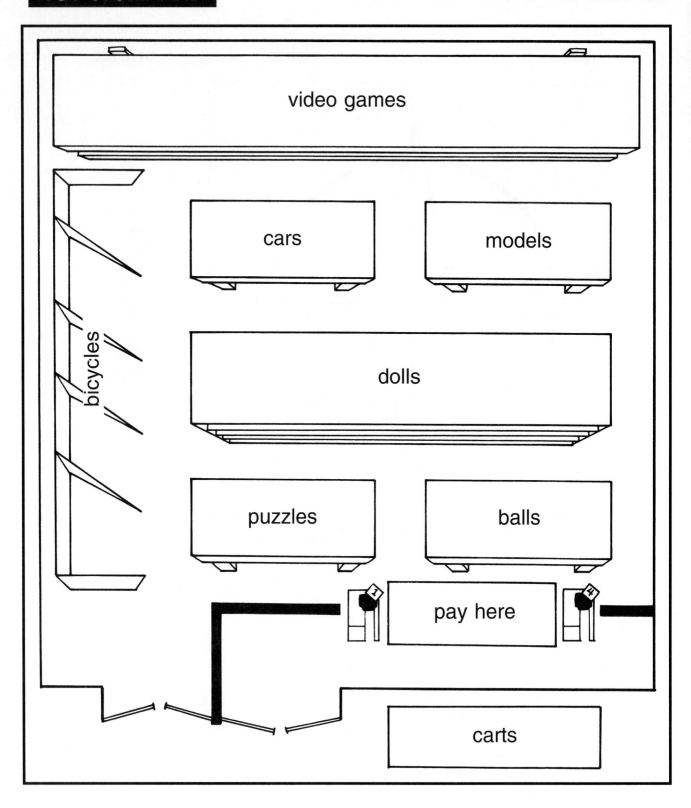

Name_____

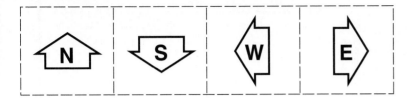

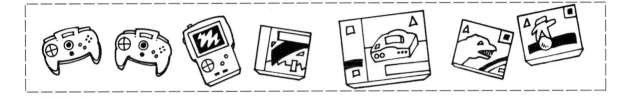

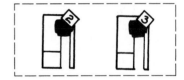

Name _____

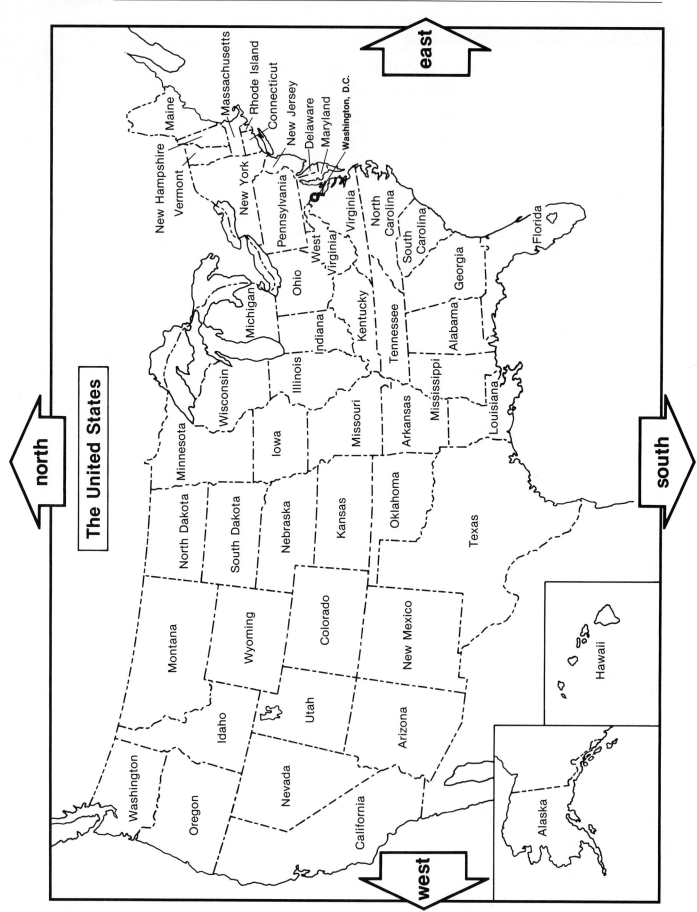

east

north

The United States

south

west

Maine

Massachusetts

Rhode Island

Connecticut

New Jersey

Delaware

Maryland

Washington, D.C.

New Hampshire

Vermont

New York

Pennsylvania

West Virginia

Virginia

North Carolina

South Carolina

Florida

Ohio

Kentucky

Tennessee

Georgia

Alabama

Michigan

Indiana

Illinois

Wisconsin

Iowa

Missouri

Arkansas

Mississippi

Louisiana

Minnesota

North Dakota

South Dakota

Nebraska

Kansas

Oklahoma

Texas

Montana

Wyoming

Colorado

New Mexico

Hawaii

Washington

Oregon

Idaho

Utah

Arizona

Nevada

California

Alaska

Maps•Globes•Graphs   Level A

Name_____

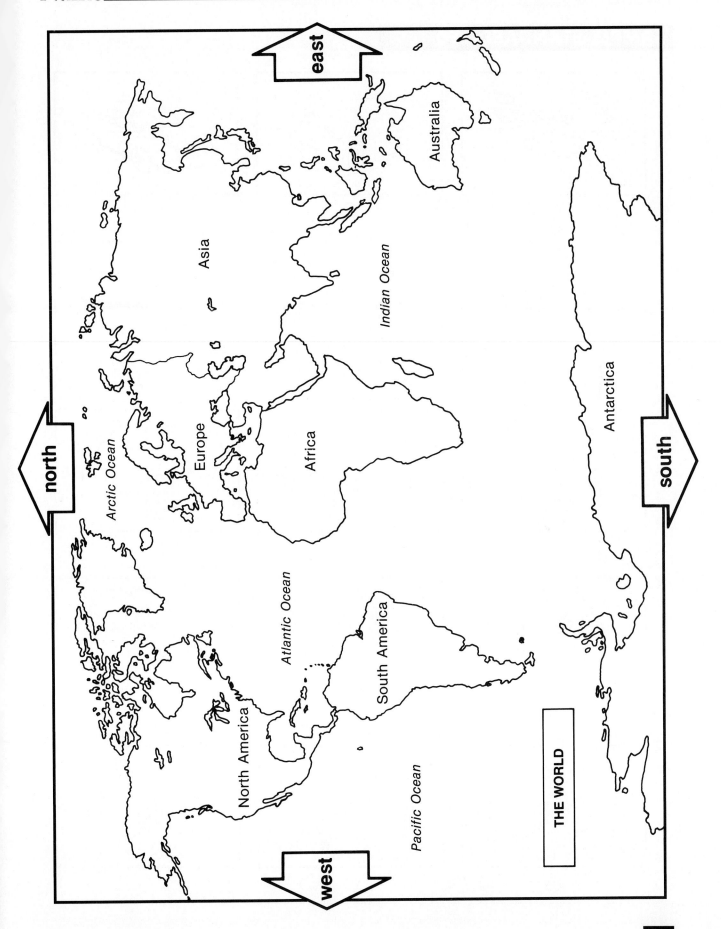

THE WORLD

Name_____

SAMPLE STANDARDIZED TEST

1.

2.

3.

4.

5.

Name_____

SAMPLE STANDARDIZED TEST

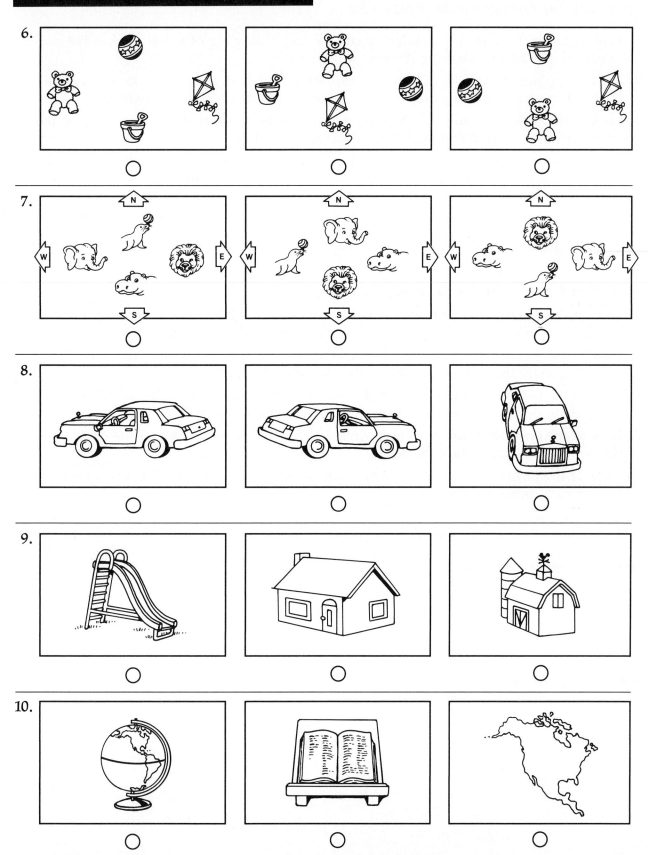

Sample Standardized Test Questions
To Be Read by Teacher to Students

Directions for Questions on Page T30

1. Look at the pictures in row 1. Which picture shows a drawing of a car? Darken the circle under the picture that shows a drawing of a car.

2. Look at the pictures in row 2. Which picture shows the way a school looks from above? Darken the circle under the picture that shows how a school looks from above.

3. Look at the pictures in row 3. Which picture shows the apple at the bottom? Darken the circle under the picture that shows the apple at the bottom.

4. Look at the pictures in row 4. Which pictures shows the girl standing to the right of the boy? Darken the circle under the picture that shows the girl standing to the right of the boy.

5. Look at the pictures in row 5. Which pictures shows the horse standing to the left of the barn? Darken the circle under the picture that shows the horse standing to the left of the barn.

Directions for Questions on Page T31

6. Look at the pictures in row 6. Which picture shows the teddy bear on the north side? Darken the circle under the picture that shows the teddy bear on the north side.

7. Look at the pictures in row 7. Which picture shows the elephant west of the lion? Darken the circle under the picture that shows the elephant west of the lion.

8. Look at the pictures in row 8. Which picture shows the car that is facing south? Darken the circle under the picture that shows the car is facing south.

9. Look at the symbols in row 9. Which symbol stands for a house? Darken the circle under the symbol that stands for a house.

10. Look at the pictures in row 10. Which picture shows a globe? Darken the circle under the picture that shows a globe.

Answers appear below.

Page T30	Page T31
1. ○ ○ ●	6. ○ ● ○
2. ○ ○ ●	7. ● ○ ○
3. ○ ● ○	8. ○ ○ ●
4. ● ○ ○	9. ○ ● ○
5. ● ○ ○	10. ● ○ ○

Maps
Globes
Graphs

Level A

Writer
Henry Billings

Consultants

Marian Gregory
Teacher
San Luis Coastal Unified School District
San Luis Obispo, California

Gloria Sesso
Supervisor of Social Studies
Half Hollow Hills School District
Dix Hills, New York

Norman McRae, Ph.D.
Former Director of Fine Arts and Social
Studies
Detroit Public Schools
Detroit, Michigan

Edna Whitfield
Former Social Studies Supervisor
St. Louis Public Schools
St. Louis, Missouri

Marilyn Nebenzahl
Social Studies Consultant
San Francisco, California

Karen Wiggins
Director of Social Studies
Richardson Independent School District
Richardson, Texas

Check the Maps•Globes•Graphs Website to find more fun geography activities at home.

Go to www.HarcourtAchieve.com/mggwelcome.html

Harcourt Achieve

Rigby • Steck-Vaughn

www.HarcourtAchieve.com
1.800.531.5015

Acknowledgments

Cartography	Land Registration and Information Service
	Amherst, Nova Scotia, Canada
	Gary J. Robinson
	MapQuest.com, Inc.
	R.R. Donnelley and Sons Company
	XNR Productions Inc., Madison, Wisconsin

Photography Credits

COVER (globe, clouds), pp. 4, 5 (both), 6 (both), 8 © PhotoDisc; pp. 12, 13 David McKenzie; pp. 16, 17 Stan Kearl; p. 21 © Graphic Eye/Tony Stone Images; p. 22 David Phillips; p. 24 David Phillips; p. 25 Gary Russ; p. 27 © Mark Segal/TSW-Click/Chicago; p. 30 David McKenzie; p. 36 David McKenzie; p. 44 (t) © Larry Lefever/Grant Heilman Photography; p. 44 (b) Stan Kearl; p. 52 © Index Stock International, Inc.; p. 52 (inset) David McKenzie; p. 63 © PhotoDisc

Illustration Credits

David Griffin pp. 9, 10, 14, 15, 21, 23, 25, 28, 29, 42, 50; Michael Krone pp. 18, 19, 20, 37, 38, 41; T.K. Riddle pp. 31, 32, 33, 34, 35, 44, 45, 46, 47, 48; Rusty Kaim p. 4

ISBN 0-7398-9101-4

Contents

Geography Themes

Geography is the study of Earth and its people.
We can tell about geography in five ways.

- **Location**
- **Place**
- **Human/Environment Interaction**
- **Movement**
- **Regions**

Location tells where something is.
It tells what something is near.

Kami lives in an apartment.
It is in a big city.
It is near a park.

1. What is near your home?

_____

Answers will vary. Accept all reasonable answers.

_____

_____

Place tells what a location is like.

Lara lives in a crowded city.
The buildings are very close together.
There are no trees or grassy yards.

2. What is it like where you live?

Answers will vary. Accept all reasonable answers.

Human/Environment Interaction tells how people
  live in a place.

Casey lives on a horse farm.
His family uses the land to raise
  horses.
Casey likes to help with the
  horses.

3. How do people use the land where you live?

Answers will vary. Accept all reasonable answers.

Movement tells how people get from place to place.

Hana and Miki walk to school.
Some days they ride their bicycles.

4. How do you get to school?

Answers will vary. Accept all reasonable answers.

Regions tell how parts of Earth are alike.

Katrina lives in a mountain
   region.
The winters are very cold.
The mountains are covered
   with snow.

5. Do you live on flat land, a hill, or a mountain?

_____

Answers will vary. Accept all reasonable answers.

Draw a picture of the place where you live.

6. Circle the name of your favorite time of the year.

Fall   Winter   Spring   Summer

7. What is your favorite season like?

_____

Answers will vary. Accept all reasonable answers.

This is a **photo**.

It is a picture made by a .

Name _____

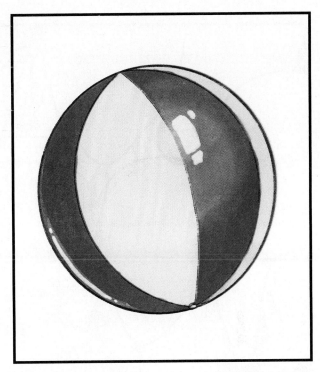

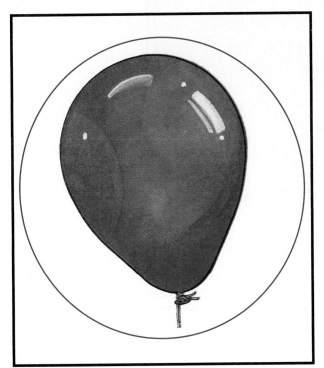

These are **drawings**.
Which drawings are of things in the photo?
Circle them.

Finding Things in a Picture

This is a drawing of the photo.
It shows the same place.

1. Color the balloons.

2. Color the hat.

3. Color the cake.

Finding Things in a Picture

This drawing shows a house.

1. Color the doors brown. **Colored to match the directions**

2. Color the trees green.

3. Color the steps yellow.

Match a Photo and a Drawing

Color the rest of the drawing. Colors similar to the photo
Match the colors you see in the photo.

Name _____

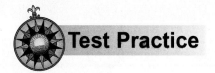

Skill Check

Words I Know   **photo   drawing**

Write each word under a picture.

_____   _____

- - - - - - - - - - - - - - - -   - - - - - - - - - - - - - - - -

photo   drawing

Reading a Picture

1. Color the house yellow. **Colored to match the directions**

2. Color the bicycle red.

3. Color the car blue.

Movement tells how people and goods get from one place to another. People and goods can move in an airplane, a train, a truck, or a ship.

1. Draw a line and match each word with its picture.

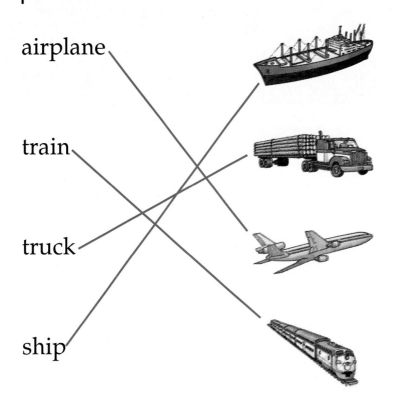

airplane

train

truck

ship

2. What is another way people and goods move?

_____

- -

walking, by car, boat, bicycle, subway

_____

Sometimes movement means how ideas are spread. We get ideas from a newspaper. We get ideas from television.

3. Look at the drawing.
    Circle the ways to get ideas.

This photo shows a park.
It was taken from the ground.
What things do you see?

Name _____

This photo shows the same park.
It was taken from above.
What else do you see?

Finding Things in a Picture

This drawing shows the same park.

1. Color the trees and grass green. **Colored to match the directions**
2. Color the pool blue.
3. Color the swing yellow.
4. Color the fence brown.

Name _____

Finding Things in a Picture

What does this drawing show?

1. Color the bed blue. **Colored to match the directions**

2. Color the table yellow.

3. Color the books green.

4. Color the toys red.

Finding Things in a Picture

What does this drawing show?

1. Color the bus yellow. **Colored to match the directions**

2. Color one car red.

3. Color two cars blue.

4. Color the truck orange.

Name _____

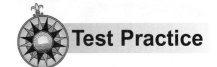

Skill Check

Color the kites in the sky. Colors similar to the photo
Match the colors you see in the photo.

This photo shows a neighborhood.
What do you see in the photo?

Name _____

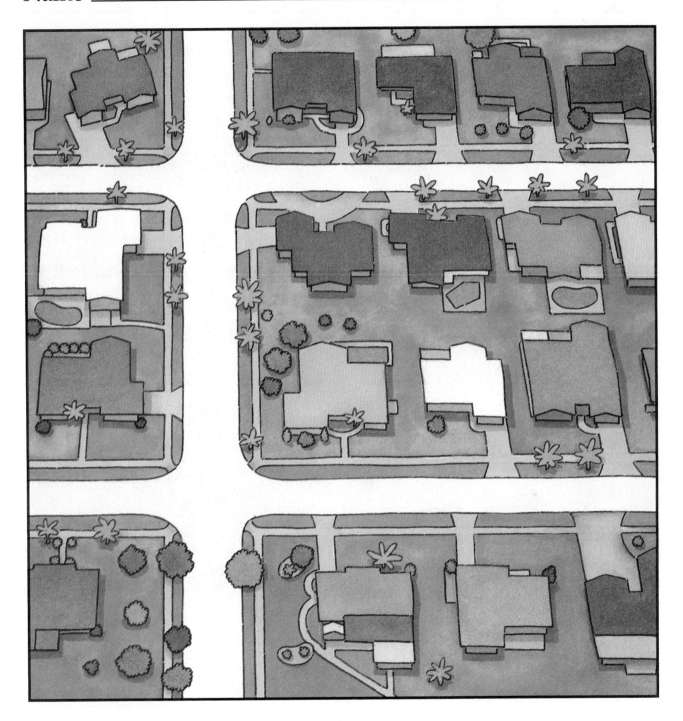

Here is the same neighborhood.
This is a **map.**

Colored to match the directions

1. Two houses are not colored. Color them yellow.

2. Find the streets. Color them gray.

Making a Map From a Photo

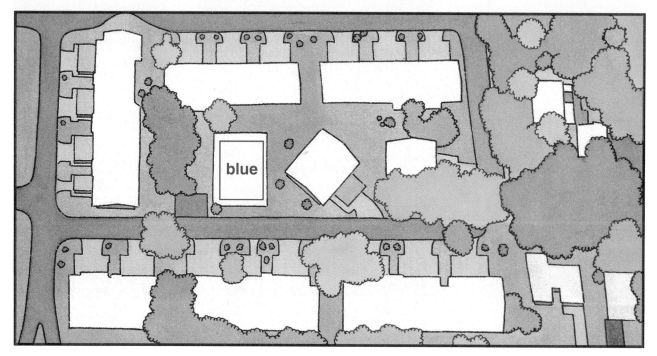

blue

1. Draw the pool on the map. Color it blue.

2. Color the rest of the map. Colors similar to the photo
   Match the colors you see in the photo.

Name _____

Making a Map From a Photo

1. Some cars are missing on the map.
   Add them to the map.

2. Color the rest of the map. **Colors similar to the photo**
   Match the colors you see in the photo.

Finding Things on a Map

This map shows a pet store.

1. Color the fish orange. **Colored to match the directions**
2. Color the dog brown.
3. Add a turtle to the map.
4. Color the turtles green.

Name _____

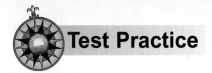

Skill Check

Words I Know   **map**

Write the word <u>map</u> under the map.
Write the word <u>photo</u> under the photo.

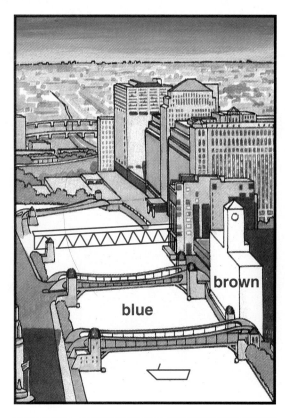

brown

blue

        photo   map

1. Look at the map. Color the building brown.

2. Add the boat to the map. **Colored and drawn to match the directions**

3. Add the bridge to the map.

4. Color the water blue.

Geography Themes Up Close

Place tells what it is like somewhere. Some places have many trees. Some places have many buildings.

1. Draw a line and match each place name with its picture.

city

park

farm

store

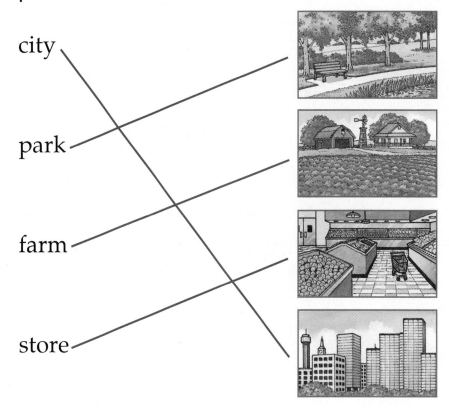

2. What is another kind of place?

_____

- -

house, school, neighborhood

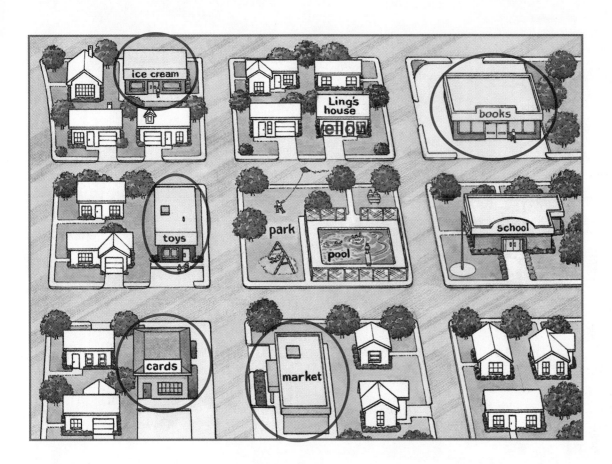

This map shows a place. It is Ling's neighborhood.
It shows what it is like in Ling's neighborhood.
There are houses, streets, and stores.

3. Color Ling's house yellow.

4. Circle the stores.

5. Name one other thing in Ling's neighborhood.

_____

Any of the following: school, park, trees, other houses, sidewalks,

driveways, specific store
_____

This photo has four sides.

The chalkboard is at the **top**.

The desks are at the **bottom**.

The flag is at the **right**.

The globe is at the **left**.

Name _____

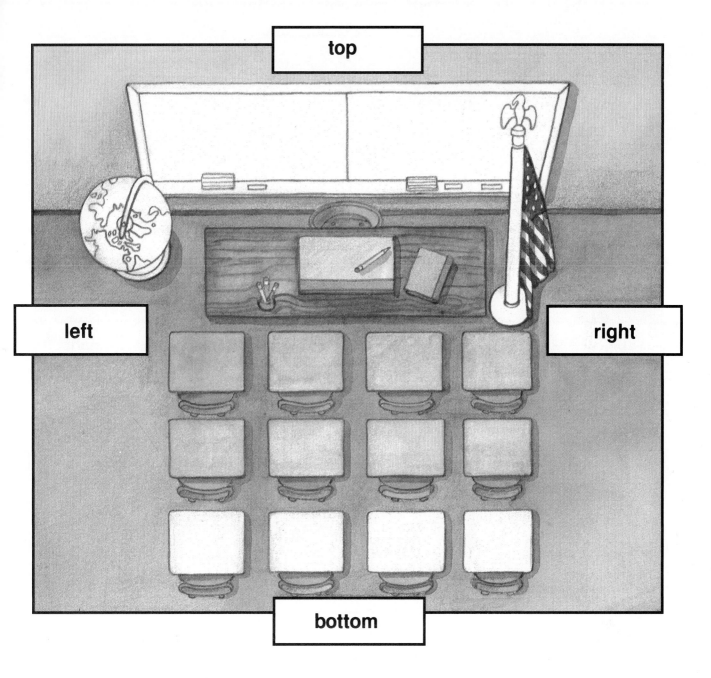

top

left

right

bottom

This is a map of a classroom.

Colored to match the directions

1. Color the chalkboard at the top green.

2. Color the desks at the bottom yellow.

3. Color the flagpole at the right red.

4. Color the globe at the left blue.

Finding Four Sides

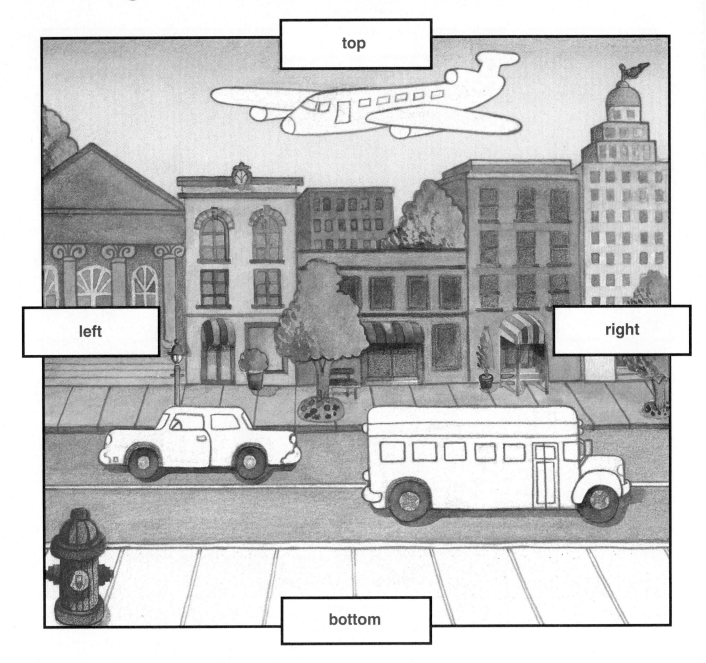

1. Write <u>top</u>, <u>bottom</u>, <u>right</u> and <u>left</u> in the boxes.
2. Color the plane at the top red. **Colored to match the directions**
3. Color the sidewalk at the bottom brown.
4. Color the bus on the right yellow.
5. Color the car on the left green.

Name _____

Finding Four Sides

1. Write top, bottom, right and left in the boxes.
2. Color two lions near the top yellow. **Colored to match the directions**
3. Color three monkeys near the bottom brown.
4. Color one elephant near the right gray.
5. Color four parrots near the left green.

Moving Toward Top, Bottom, Right, or Left

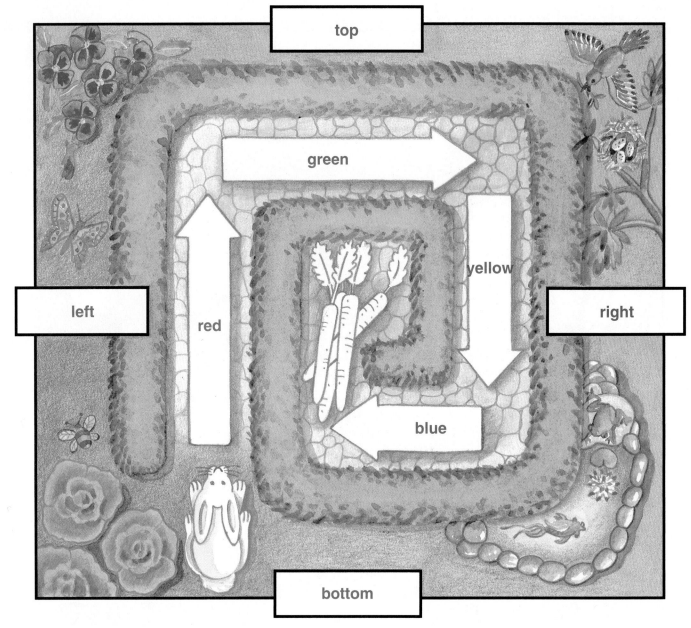

1. Write <u>top</u>, <u>bottom</u>, <u>right</u> and <u>left</u> in the boxes.
2. One arrow points to the top. Color it red. **Colored to match the directions**
3. One arrow points to the right. Color it green.
4. One arrow points to the bottom. Color it yellow.
5. One arrow points to the left. Color it blue.
6. Color the carrots.

Name _____

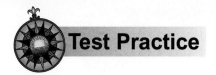

Skill Check

Words I Know   **top**   **bottom**   **right**   **left**

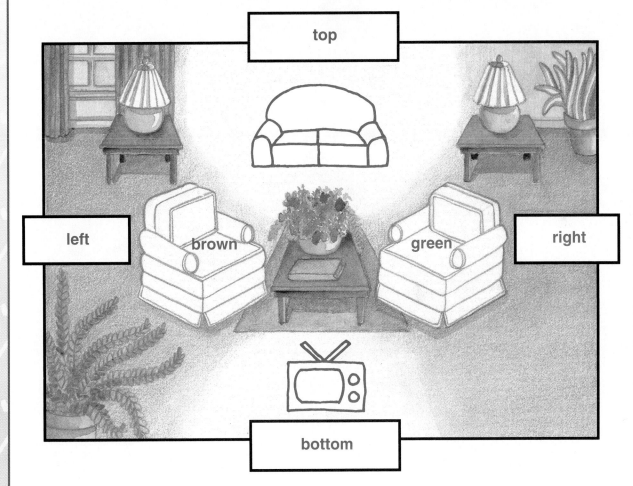

This map shows a living room.

1. Write <u>top</u>, <u>bottom</u>, <u>right</u> and <u>left</u> in the boxes.
2. Draw a sofa near the top.
3. Draw a TV near the bottom.
4. Color the chair near the right green.
5. Color the chair near the left brown.

North, south, east, and west are **directions**.
<u>N</u>, <u>S</u>, <u>E</u>, and <u>W</u> stand for north, south, east, and west.

The girl faces **north**. Find <u>N</u> in the photo.
South is behind her. Find <u>S</u> in the photo.
East is to her right. Find <u>E</u> in the photo.
West is to her left. Find <u>W</u> in the photo.

Name _____

This map shows a farm.
The top of the map is north.

Where is each thing?
Write north, south, east, and west.

north

east

west

south

Finding Directions at the Fruit Market

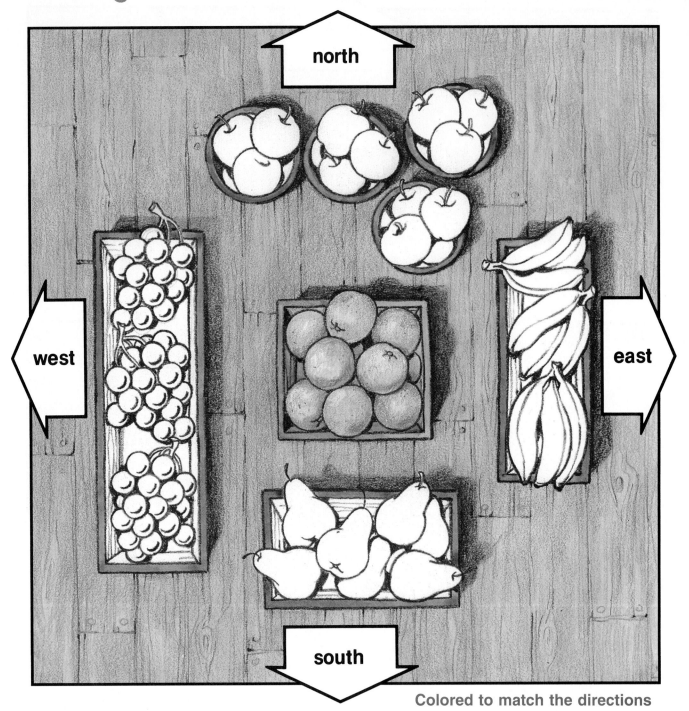

Colored to match the directions

1. Which fruit is on the north side? Color it red. apples—north
2. Which fruit is on the south side? Color it green. pears—south
3. Which fruit is on the east side? Color it yellow. bananas—east
4. Which fruit is on the west side? Color it purple. grapes—west

Name _____

Finding Directions at the Park

Start at the flower gardens.
Draw an arrow to show where you go.
Then circle the letter of the direction you go.

1. Go to feed the . You go (N) E .

2. Next go to the . You go S (W) .

3. Then go to the . You go (S) N .

4. Now run to the . You run W (E) .

Finding Directions at the Fair

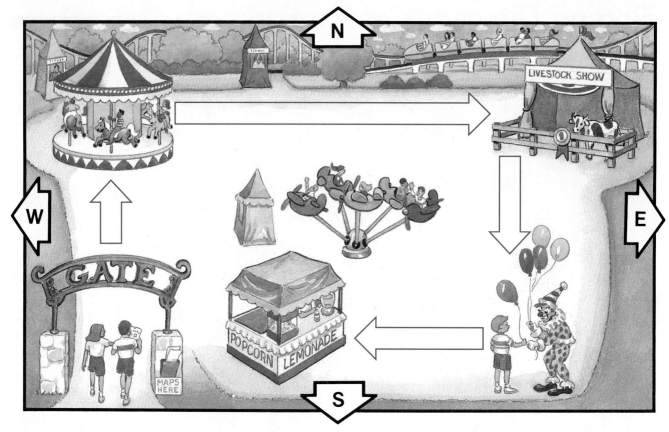

Get a map at the gate and have fun at the fair.
Draw an arrow to show where you go.
Write the direction you go to get

① from GATE to 🎠 . _____ N or north

② from 🎠 to LIVESTOCK SHOW . _____ E or east

③ from LIVESTOCK SHOW to 🤡 . _____ S or south

④ from 🤡 to POPCORN LEMONADE . _____ W or west

Name _____

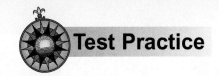

Skill Check

Words I Know   **north**   **south**   **east**   **west**

Finding Directions on a Map

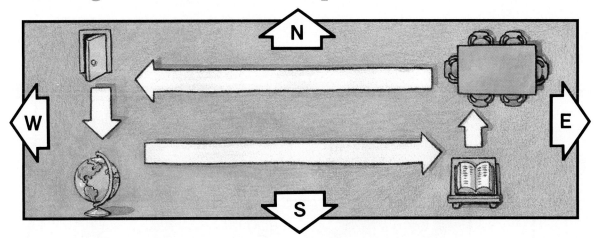

This map shows a library.

Write the direction that tells the way to get

① from to .   south

② from to .   east

③ from to .   north

④ from to .   west

Regions are areas that are alike. Regions can be large like mountain regions.

Regions can be small. Parts of a room can be a region. This map shows a classroom.

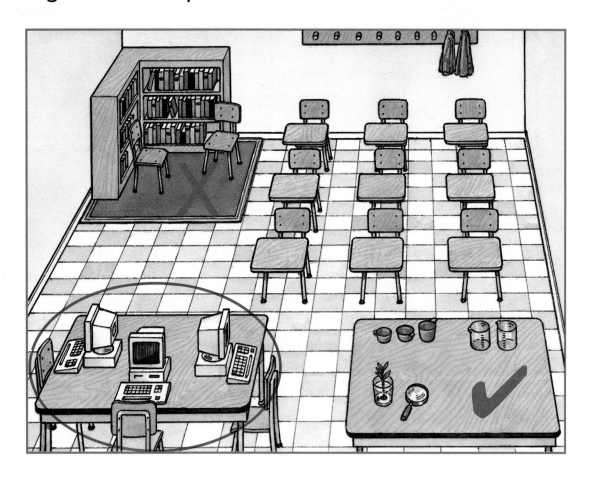

1. Put a ✔ on the science region.

2. Draw a circle around the computer region.

3. Draw an X on the reading region.

4. Where is each region? Write <u>north</u>, <u>south</u>, <u>east</u>, or <u>west</u>.

park _____ south _____   forest _____ west _____

houses _____ east _____   stores _____ north _____

Symbols and Map Keys

The photo shows a real barn.
The drawing is a **symbol** for a barn.
A symbol stands for something real.

Match each symbol with a photo.

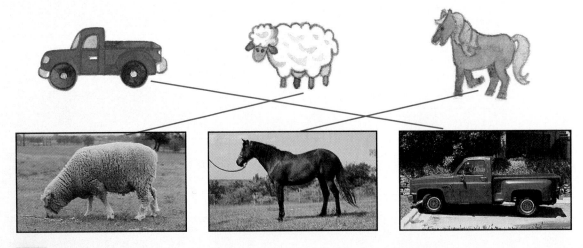

Name _____

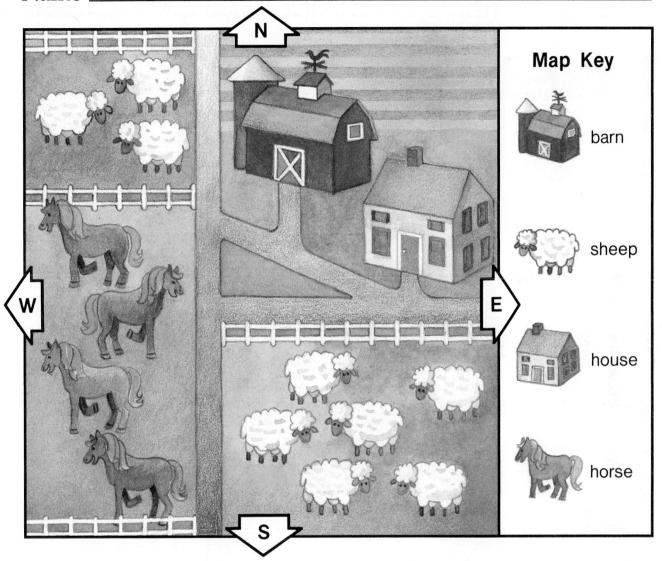

This map shows a farm.
The **map key** tells what each symbol stands for.

Write what the symbols stand for.
The first one is done for you.

Finding Symbols on a Map

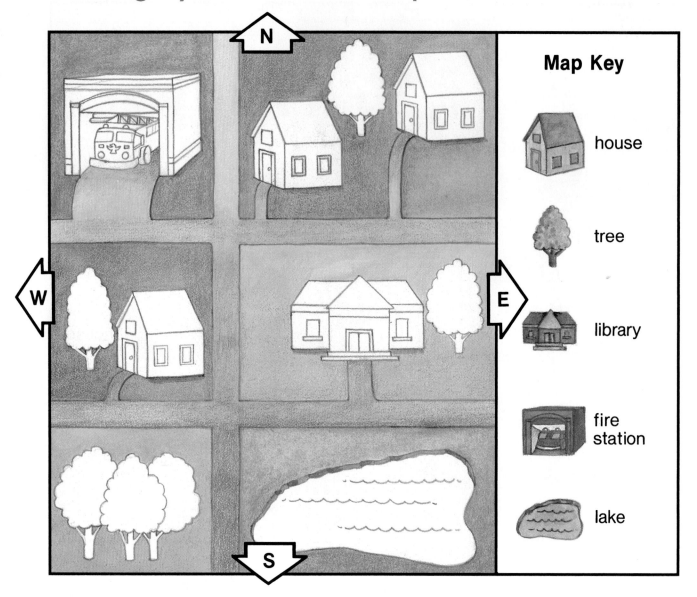

1. Find <u>N</u>, <u>S</u>, <u>E</u>, and <u>W</u> on the map.
2. Study the map key.
3. Find the trees on the map. Color them green.
4. Find the houses. Color them yellow.   **Colored to match the directions**
5. Find the library. Color it brown.
6. Find the fire station. Color it red.
7. Find the lake. Color it blue.

Name _____

Finding Symbols on a Map

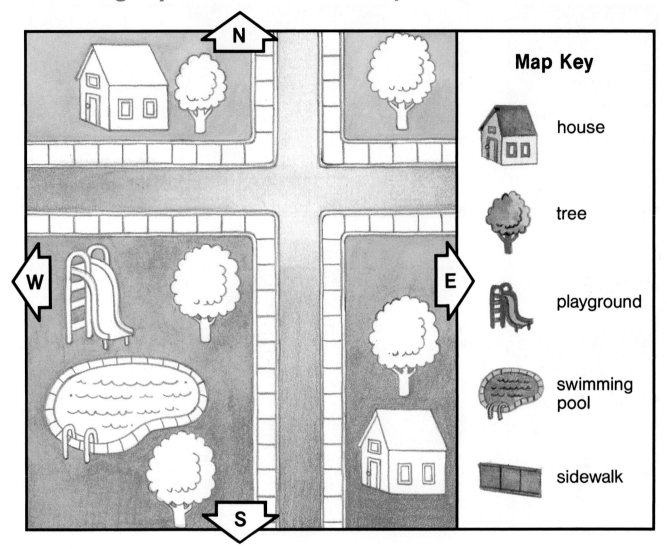

Map Key

house

tree

playground

swimming pool

sidewalk

1. Find <u>N</u>, <u>S</u>, <u>E</u>, and <u>W</u> on the map.

2. Study the map key.

3. Find the houses on the map. Color them yellow.

4. Find the trees. Color them green. **Colored to match the directions**

5. Find the playground. Color it red.

6. Find the swimming pool. Color it blue.

7. Find the sidewalks. Color them brown.

Finding Symbols on a Map

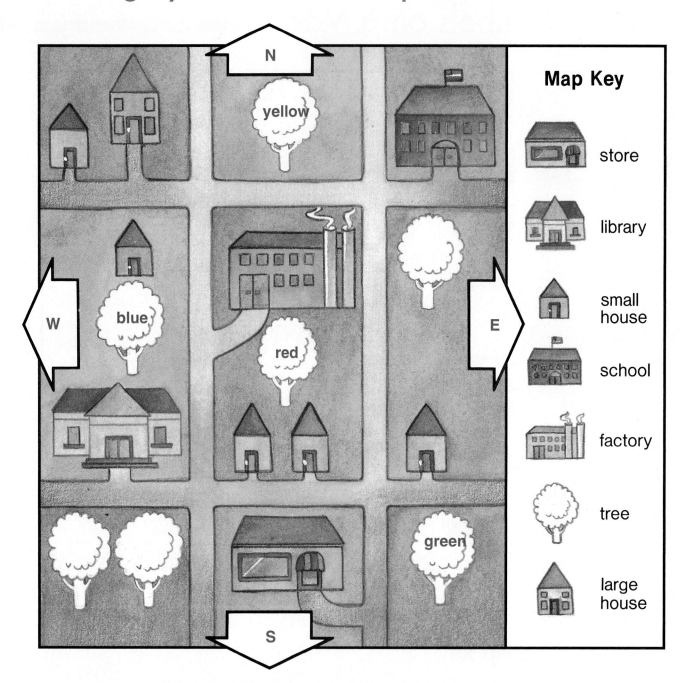

1. Write <u>N</u>, <u>S</u>, <u>E</u>, and <u>W</u> where they belong.
2. Find the factory. Go south. Color that tree red.
3. Find the library. Go north. Color that tree blue.
4. Find the store. Go east. Color that tree green.
5. Find the school. Go west. Color that tree yellow.

Name _____

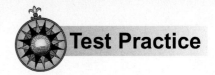

Skill Check

Words I Know   **symbol**   **map key**

_____

- - - - - - - - - - - - - - - - -

The _____map key_____ tells what each symbol stands for.

Reading a Map

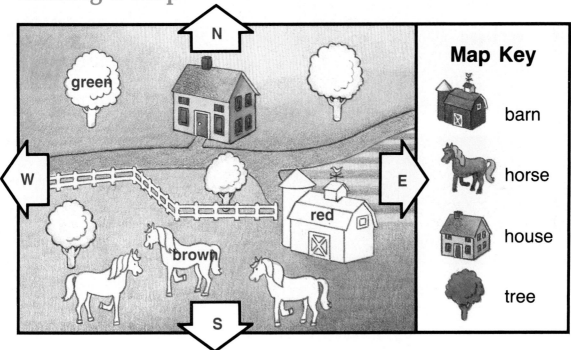

This map shows a farm.

1. Write <u>N</u>, <u>S</u>, <u>E</u>, and <u>W</u> where they belong.
2. Find the horses. Color them brown.
3. Find the barn. Color it red.
4. Find the house. Go west. Color that tree green.

Geography Themes Up Close

Human/Environment Interaction tells how people use the land where they live. They use rivers for water. They grow food on the land.

1. Match each picture with a sentence.

People build houses on the land.

People have fun in parks.

People use grass to feed animals.

People fish in lakes.

Sometimes people change the land. They build roads and bridges. They build houses or farms on the land.

2. Draw pictures that show how people change the land.

People build tall buildings.   People farm the land.

3. How have people changed the land where you live?

_____

_____

_____

_____

The large photo shows **Earth**.
Earth is round like a ball.

The small photo shows a **globe**.
A globe is also round like a ball.
A globe is a **model** of Earth.

Name _____

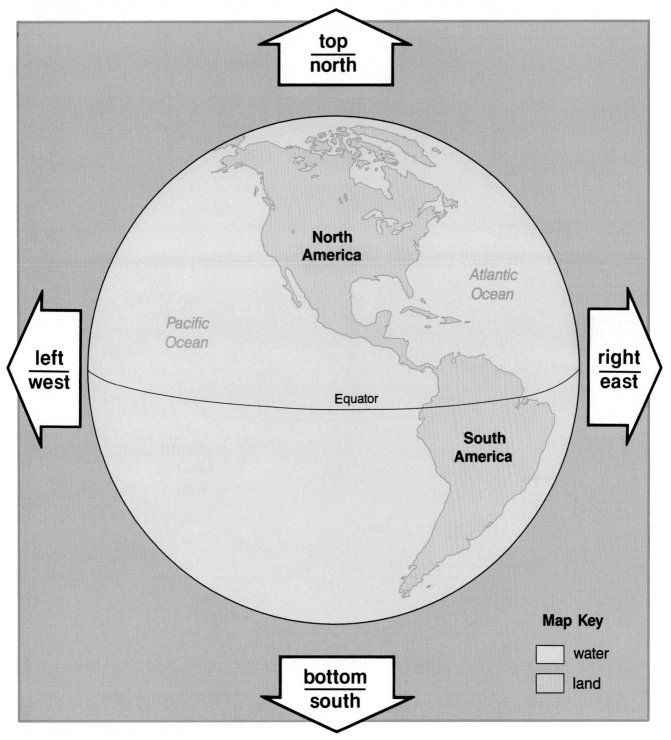

Look at the globe above.
The blue color stands for water.
The green color stands for land.
The words are names of real places.

Finding Places on a Globe

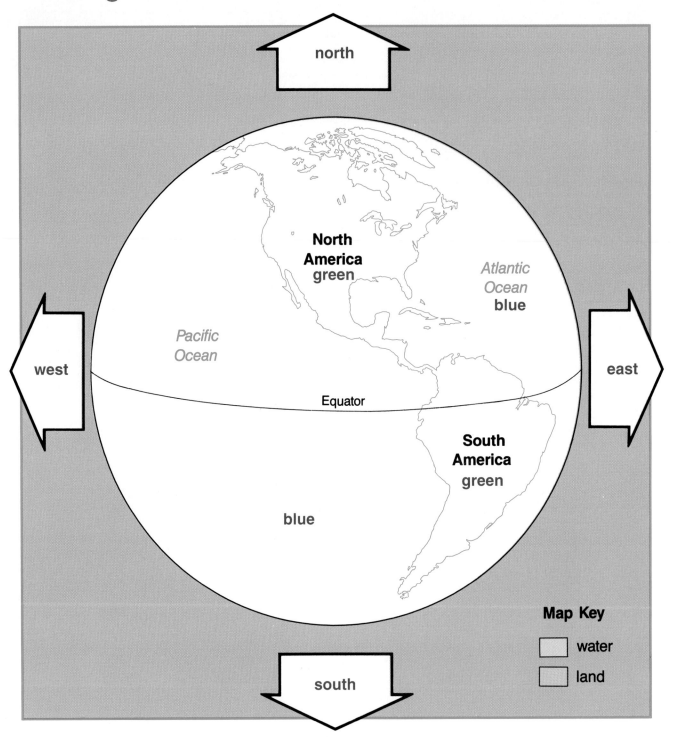

1. Write <u>north</u>, <u>south</u>, <u>east</u>, and <u>west</u> in the arrows.
2. Color the water blue.
3. Color the land green.

Name _____

Finding Places on a Globe

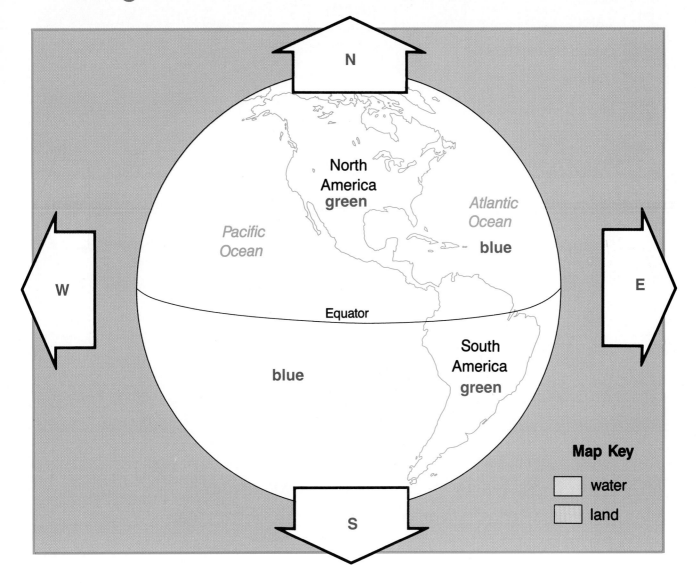

1. Write <u>N</u>, <u>S</u>, <u>E</u>, and <u>W</u> in the arrows.
2. Color the globe to match the map key.   **Colors similar to the map key**
3. Look at the land on the map.
4. Find the water to the east of the land.

   _____

   _ _ _ _ _ _ _ _ _ _ _ _ _ _ _

5. It is called the Atlantic _____Ocean_____.

Finding Places on a Globe

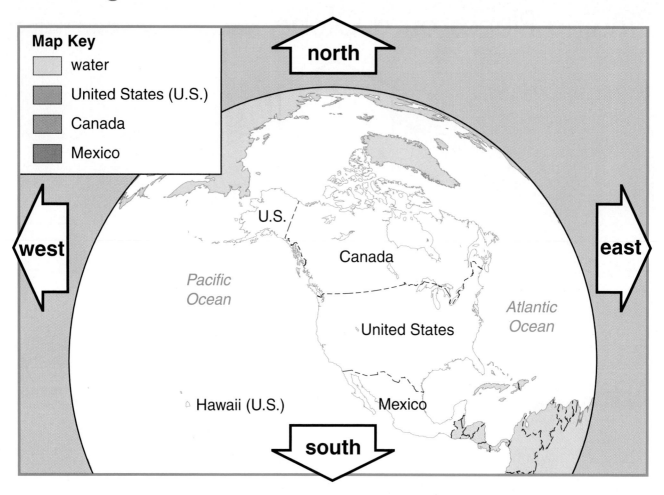

Map Key
- water
- United States (U.S.)
- Canada
- Mexico

north

west

east

U.S.

Canada

Pacific Ocean

United States

Atlantic Ocean

Hawaii (U.S.)

Mexico

south

The United States is part of North America.
Mexico and Canada are also in North America.

1. What country is south of the United States?

_____

- -

Mexico
_____

2. What country is north of the United States?

_____

- -

Canada
_____

3. Color the map to match the map key. **Colors similar to the map key**

Name _____

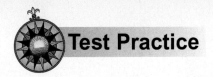

Skill Check

Words I Know **globe** **model**

_____

- - - - - - - - - - - - - - -

A _____ globe _____ looks like Earth.

Reading a Globe

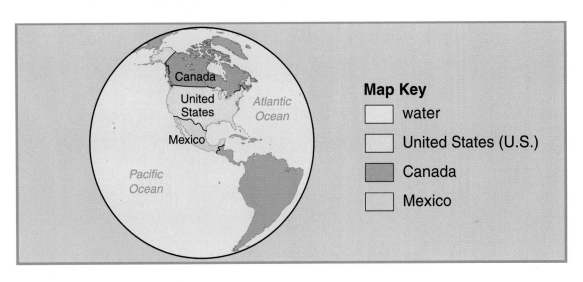

_____

- - - - - - - - - - - - - - -

1. The Atlantic Ocean is _____ east _____
   of the United States.

   _____

   - - - - - - - - - - - - -

2. Canada is _____ north _____ of the United States.

   _____

   - - - - - - - - - - - - -

3. Mexico is _____ south _____ of the United States.

Geography Themes Up Close

Location tells where places are found. Every place on Earth has a location. Iowa is in the United States. It is west of Illinois.

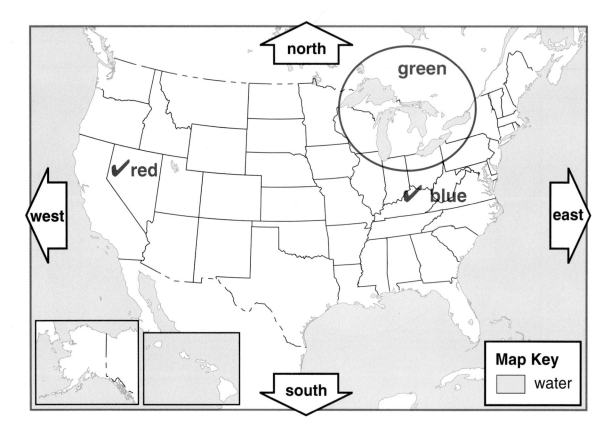

1. There are high mountains in the west.
   Put a red ✔ in the west.

2. There are many rivers in the east.
   Put a blue ✔ in the east.

3. There are some big lakes in the north.
   Circle the lakes in green.

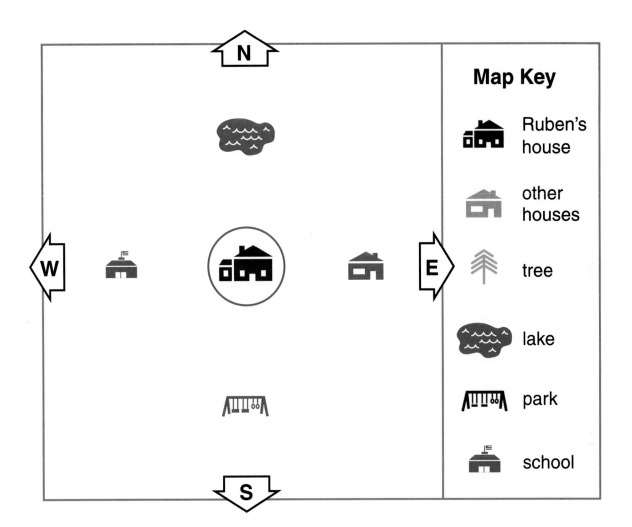

Look at the map of Ruben's neighborhood. Find Ruben's house. Circle it. Draw the rest of the map.

4. Draw a house east of Ruben's house.

5. Draw a lake north of Ruben's house.

6. Draw a park south of Ruben's house.

7. Draw a school west of Ruben's house.

west

Washington

Oregon

Idaho

Montana

North Dakota

South Dakota

Wyoming

Nebraska

Nevada

Utah

Colorado

Kansas

California

Arizona

New Mexico

O

Texas

Alaska

Hawaii

north

The United States

New Hampshire

Maine

Vermont

Minnesota

Michigan

New York

Wisconsin

Massachusetts

Rhode Island

Connecticut

Pennsylvania

New Jersey

Iowa

Ohio

Delaware

Illinois

Indiana

Washington, D.C.

Maryland

West Virginia

Virginia

east

Missouri

Kentucky

North Carolina

Tennessee

Arkansas

South Carolina

Alabama

Georgia

Mississippi

Louisiana

Florida

south

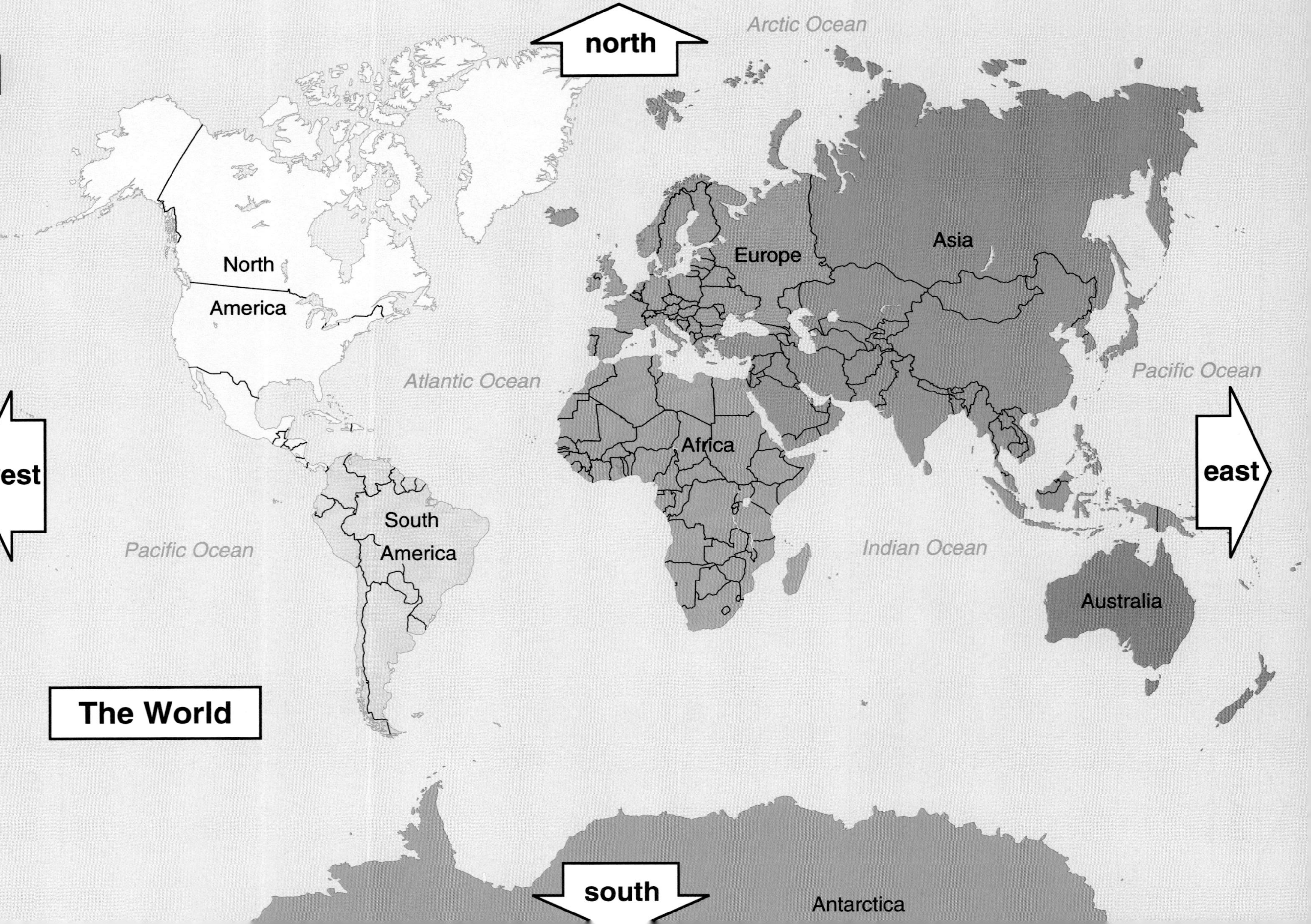
north
Arctic Ocean
The World
North
America
South
America
Europe
Asia
Africa
Australia
Antarctica
Atlantic Ocean
Pacific Ocean
Pacific Ocean
Indian Ocean
west
east
south

Glossary

bottom
page 30

Canada
page 56

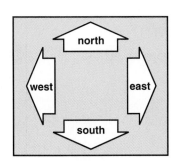

directions
page 36

drawing
page 9

Earth
page 52

east
page 36

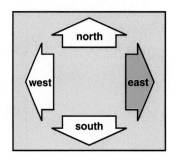

globe
page 52

left
page 30

map
page 23

map key
page 45

Mexico
page 56

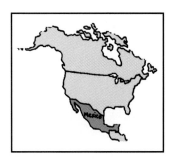

model
page 52

north
page 36

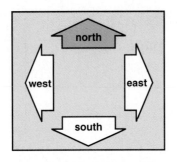

ocean
page 55

photo
page 8

right
page 30

south
page 36

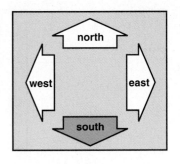

symbol
page 44

barn

top
page 30

United States
page 56

west
page 36

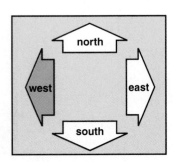